BREAKING the Mode

The Italian installation and this publication
are dedicated to Gianfranco Ferré

Kaye Durland Spilker
Sharon Sadako Takeda

BREAKING the Mode

Contemporary Fashion from the Permanent Collection
Los Angeles County Museum of Art

Contributions by
Paola Colaiacomo
Maria Luisa Frisa

SKIRA

Cover
Issey Miyake, "Minaret" Dress,
spring/summer 1994

Design
Marcello Francone

Editorial Coordination
Francesca Ruggiero

Editing
Emily Ligniti

Layout
Serena Parini

Translations
Lucian Comoy

Photo Credits
© Museum Associates,
Los Angeles County Museum of Art

First published in Italy in 2007 by
Skira Editore S.p.A.
Palazzo Casati Stampa
via Torino 61
20123 Milano
Italy
www.skira.net

Printed and bound in Italy. First edition
ISBN: 978-88-6130-301-0

Distributed in North America by Rizzoli
International Publications, Inc., 300 Park
Avenue South, New York, NY 10010, USA.
Distributed elsewhere in the world
by Thames and Hudson Ltd., 181A High
Holborn, London WC1V 7QX,
United Kingdom.

CONTROModa
La moda contemporanea della collezione permanente
del Los Angeles County Museum of Art

Florence, Palazzo Strozzi
12 October 2007 – 20 January 2008

BREAKING the Mode
Contemporary Fashion from the Permanent Collection
Los Angeles County Museum of Art

Indianapolis Museum of Art
16 March – 1 June 2008

The original exhibition,
Breaking the Mode: Contemporary Fashion from the Permanent Collection, was organized by the Los Angeles County Museum of Art, 17 September 2006 – 7 January 2007

With the patronage of
Ministero per i Beni e le Attività Culturali
Ministero degli Affari Esteri
Camera Nazionale della Moda Italiana

Promoted and Organized by
Fondazione Palazzo Strozzi, Florence

With the support of
Regione Toscana
Provincia di Firenze
Comune di Firenze
Soprintendenza Speciale per il Polo Museale Fiorentino, Galleria del Costume di Palazzo Pitti

Exhibition Concept
Los Angeles County Museum of Art

Curated by
Kaye Durland Spilker
Sharon Sadako Takeda
Los Angeles County Museum of Art

Curatorial Collaboration
Italian Edition
Maria Luisa Frisa

Advisory Board
Holly Brubach
Maria Luisa Frisa
Franca Sozzani
Kaye Durland Spilker
Sharon Sadako Takeda
Stefano Tonchi

Exhibition by
Fondazione Palazzo Strozzi, Florence

Exhibition Design
Studio Italo Rota, Milan
with Devis Venturelli

Exhibition Design Coordination
Luigi Cupellini, Florence

Exhibition Fabrication
Eurostands, Milan

Monitor Rentals and Video
Post-production
Avuelle, Florence

Head of Security
Ulderigo Frusi

Climate Control
Cristina Danti
Roberto Boddi
Opificio delle Pietre Dure, Florence

Communications and Promotion
Susanna Holm
Sigma C.S.C., Florence

Press Office
Karla Otto, Milan
Sue Bond, Suffolk - UK

Graphic Design
RovaiWeber design, Florence

Photo Campaign
Los Angeles County Museum of Art

Translations
Antonia Gargiulo

Website
Netribe

Booking and Educational Services
Sigma C.S.C., Florence

Workshops
With the contribution of The Forsythe Company, Frankfurt

Audio Guides
Antenna Audio, Italy

Shipping
Arteria, Florence

Exhibition and Ticket Office Staff
TML Service, Florence

Multichannel Ticket Office
Vivaticket by Charta

www.contromodafirenze.it

The Fondazione Palazzo Strozzi
and the Los Angeles County Museum
of Art would like to thank
Elmira Aliyakparova
Rita Airaghi
Paola Bianchi
Micaela Calabresi
Valeria Cerulli
Marco Ciatti
Danilo Cognolato
Alessia Crespi
Patrizia Cucco
Valentina D'Amato
Francesco D'Elia
Antonella Di Marco
Cecilia Desalles
Leonardo Ferragamo
Valentina Guerra
Amanda Montanari
Camilla Orlandi
Elena Paganini
Laudomia Pucci
Giorgio Re
Paola Sacchi
Verde Visconti
Angela Ward
Antonella Zunino

Many thanks also to
Holly Brubach
Mariuccia Casadio
Giusi Ferré
Albertina Marzotto
Suzy Menkes
Franca Sozzani
for their contribution.

We are especially grateful
to Emilio Pucci for the scarves
and ties worn by the staff during
the exhibition.

Technical Sponsors

APT Firenze
ATAF
Firenze dei Teatri
Firenze Parcheggi
Fondazione Teatro del Maggio
Musicale Fiorentino
Starhotels
Toscana Promozione

Main Sponsor

LACMA

FONDAZIONE
PALAZZO
STROZZI

Breaking the Mode: Contemporary Fashion from the Permanent Collection, Los Angeles County Museum of Art *examines the far-reaching changes that have taken place in clothing design during the past three decades. Utilizing the rich holdings of LACMA's Department of Costume and Textiles, the exhibition was organized by curator Kaye Durland Spilker and senior curator and department head Sharon Sadako Takeda, with the collaboration of curatorial assistants Michelle Webb Fandrich and Melinda Webber Kerstein. Organized into four thematic sections— construction, materials, form, and concept—* Breaking the Mode *focuses on the myriad of innovative methods that designers have used to turn fashion completely upside down and inside out. Through reinterpreting historical elements in surprisingly new ways, harnessing modern technology, and pushing the boundaries of conventional norms of dress, contemporary fashion designers have tackled the same issues as contemporary painters and sculptors. This exhibition beautifully brings these issues to the forefront and confirms their importance.*

The original exhibition opened with great fanfare and generated much excitement and interest throughout its installation in the fall of 2006 at LACMA. It is gratifying to know that the exhibition will now be seen by an international audience as ControModa: La moda contemporanea della collezione permanente del Los Angeles County Museum of Art. *LACMA would like to thank the Fondazione Palazzo Strozzi in Florence, Italy, and its Director James M. Bradburne for initiating the tour of* Breaking the Mode *and this publication. We are also grateful to the Indianapolis Museum of Art and its Melvin and Bren Simon Director and CEO, Maxwell L. Anderson, for bringing this intellectually stimulating exhibition to another venue in the United States.*

The challenge of coordinating and installing a major costume exhibition was skillfully met by numerous talented staff members at LACMA, whose names are listed in this volume separately. We are appreciative and proud of their work. LACMA's Steven Oliver deserves special commendation for the numerous hours he spent tirelessly creating beautiful photographs for this catalogue.

The presentation of Breaking the Mode *at LACMA was generously sponsored by the museum's Costume Council. Over the years the Costume Council has steadfastly supported the Department of Costume and Textiles in many ways, especially with programming and acquisitions. We are indebted to the Council as well as its individual members who, together with private collectors and fashion designers, have donated the works of art seen in* Breaking the Mode. *Their lasting contributions have made LACMA's costume and textiles collection one of the strongest in the United States.*

Michael Govan
Chief Executive Officer and
Wallis Annenberg Director,
Los Angeles County Museum of Art

Fashion is inseparable from the Italian identity, and Florence is the city in which fashion's Italian identity was first affirmed and given international exposure when visionary businessman Giovanni Battista Giorgini hosted the first exhibition of Italian high fashion in 1951. The Palazzo Strozzi has a long history of involvement with Italian fashion: it provided the backdrop for some of Life *magazine's most striking fashion photographs of the 1950s and hosted exhibitions of Salvatore Ferragamo in 1985 and Roberto Capucci in 1990, as well as* La Sala Bianca, nascita della moda italiana *in 1992. Now, in 2007, fashion returns to the Palazzo Strozzi with* ControModa, *an exhibition of innovative contemporary fashion that changed the face of fashion itself. Why has the Fondazione Palazzo Strozzi chosen this exhibition to follow the success of its inaugural show,* Cézanne in Florence? *For two reasons: first, to underline our commitment to contemporary culture, in which fashion plays a major role, and second, to signal a willingness to open the Palazzo Strozzi to a wide variety of audiences with a wide variety of interests.*

The exhibition ControModa *features works from the permanent collection of the Los Angeles County Museum of Art (LACMA). The exhibition was organized by LACMA curators Kaye Spilker and Sharon Takeda, and originally opened as* Breaking the Mode *at the Los Angeles County Museum of Art in September 2006 highlighting the innovations of international designers in the 1980s and 1990s. The Palazzo Strozzi installation was coordinated by curator Maria Luisa Frisa in consultation with Holly Brubach, Franca Sozzani, and Stefano Tonchi, and shows how Italian designers, too, had been blazing new trails in contemporary fashion. A series of recent additions to LACMA's collection sheds further light on the creativity of Italian fashion in the last three decades and completes the picture of how fashion continues to respond to the social, political, and cultural changes of the times.*

ControModa is deeply rooted to its time and place. ControModa is the centerpiece of a Florentine fashion season that traditionally begins in mid-June with Pitti Uomo and finishes with Pitti Uomo in January. Throughout this extended season, the Fondazione is promoting and hosting events that link all of Florence's fashion players, in order to shine a spotlight on the creativity, vitality, and innovation of fashion "Made in Italy"—and born in Florence. The Palazzo Strozzi is committed to bringing international quality cultural events to Florence, and ControModa is an expression of the Fondazione's ambitions.

In addition to all the professionals who helped bring ControModa to Florence, the Los Angeles County Museum of Art, its Director Michael Govan and its staff, and the Director of the Indianapolis Museum of Art, Maxwell L. Anderson, who will be hosting the exhibition after it leaves Florence, the Fondazione Palazzo Strozzi would especially like to thank the exhibition's public and private partners and sponsors, including the Regione Toscana, the Province of Florence, the City of Florence, and the Florentine Chamber of Commerce, all of whom strongly supported the exhibition from the outset. We would also like to thank the Cassa di Risparmio di Firenze, as well as the Association of Private Partners of the Palazzo Strozzi, who generously provided both moral and financial support at every stage of the development of the exhibition. Finally I would like to thank the entire Fondazione Palazzo Strozzi team—its Board of Trustees, its Advisory Board, its Director James M. Bradburne, and his staff—for having worked so hard to create an exhibition that gives real meaning to the slogan "think global, and act local." ControModa certainly does both.

Lorenzo Bini Smaghi
Chairman of the Board,
Fondazione Palazzo Strozzi

Contents

Kaye Durland Spilker

Introduction

Clothing design has undergone dramatic changes over the past thirty years. Since the late 1970s, designers have introduced subversive elements into the fashion system, examining and deconstructing its entrenched conventions and changing beliefs about what is aesthetically pleasing and stylish. *Breaking the Mode: Contemporary Fashion from the Permanent Collection, Los Angeles County Museum of Art* considers the work of those designers who revolutionized methods of garment construction or challenged the existing canons of the body's form, proportion, and fashionable silhouette. Most of the objects selected for this exhibition and its accompanying catalogue have been collected over the last twelve years; these articles of dress illustrate the visions and re-visions of creative thinkers whose work deserves to be investigated, displayed, and remembered.

Fashion, as a multifaceted social phenomenon, has captured the attention and financial resources of people for hundreds of years. Recounting fashion's trajectory from a historical perspective is the focus of a number of costume museums; this postulates a chronological and broad-based approach to collection development, but the mission, method, and purpose of collecting costume for a museum of art are somewhat different. While always interpreting fashion in its sociological and historical context, the art museum's primary enterprise is the search for objects that meet the same criteria applied to other forms of art in its collection, criteria that may or may not be present in all phases of fashion's continuum.

The acceptance of costume and fashion as art is not at issue in this book. The presence of costume, to a greater or lesser degree, in the greatest art forms of myriad cultures affirms that it exists as a critical and integral subject addressed by the artist. Curators approach contemporary costume as an intriguing form of art—variable, transitory, pregnant with possibilities, but also burdened by standard perceptions that deem its purpose to be only function or vanity. Exciting developments in fashion have occurred in the recent past that merit analysis, because, like other forms of art, they have left indelible imprints and changed the way we see.

A number of contemporary fashion designers take a conceptual approach in their work. With strategies similar to that of the fine artist, they examine conventional notions for origins—the "how" and "why" of the rules of fashion—then proceed to invalidate the rules with insidiously subtle or outrageously radical garments so firmly couched in tradition that the designers' subversions are truly startling. In rejecting the formulaic use of media and technique, they have established new aesthetic principles of fashion—in construction, materials, form, and ultimately, in the concept or meaning of clothes to the designer, wearer, and audience.

The Paris fashion establishment suffered an identity crisis around 1980 with the emergence of Japanese designers Issey Miyake, Rei Kawakubo, and Yohji Yamamoto, who challenged the venerable standards of construction and fit by suggesting a different vision for dressing the body. The fundamentals of Western European fashion have cus-

Issey Miyake
Dress from the "Rhythm Pleats" series,
spring/summer 1990 (detail)

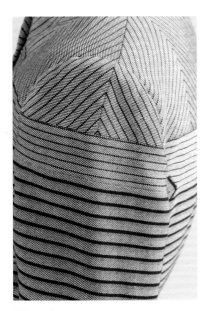

Gilbert Adrian
Two-piece Suit, 1946–1948 (detail)

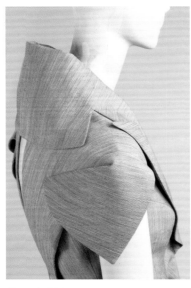

Alexander McQueen
Two-piece Suit, spring/summer 1999 (detail)

tomarily required complex methods of cutting, padding, and precise tailoring to emphasize contours of the figure. These artists, however, used the characteristics of traditional Japanese clothing to drape and wrap textiles that concealed, if not obliterated, the body's outline. Body parts were integral, but sometimes subordinate to the desired sculptural effect.

The disorder, anarchy, and perceived dishevelment of the work of these three designers was especially shocking because the fashion world was so comfortable with the formulary of traditional couture dressmaking established in the early to mid-twentieth century. In 1947, Christian Dior's first collection—proclaimed "The New Look" by the fashion press—reintroduced women to the hourglass contour that dominated late-nineteenth-century dress. The natural body did not dictate the design; constructing the garment from the inside out, the couturier sculpted the contrived body he envisioned. The achievement of the extreme proportions of this idealized shape, with its exaggerated hip and bust and minimized waist, required the tailor's sleight of hand and an element of deceit. Stitching, padding, and manipulation of the fabric through steaming and stretching were used to create a garment that did not necessarily reflect the reality of the body beneath. Multiple yards of horsehair, crinoline, netting, and tulle created elaborate understructures for the architectural ball gowns of Dior and Charles James. These elements formed the structure concealed under the finished surface.

Gowns by James and tailored suits by Jean Dessès, Gilbert Adrian, and the British firm Lachasse Ltd. (pp. 42, 36, 52–53) are consummate examples of masterful tailoring, the standard by which couture was (and is) measured. Internalizing and revising these standards, Jean Paul Gaultier, Rei Kawakubo, Alexander McQueen, and John Galliano (pp. 47, 57, 55, 54) paid homage to the antecedents, but rethought them from a contemporary perspective—either by revising the expected silhouette or by flouting the conventional definition of textiles appropriate to elegance and opulent display. Issey Miyake and Dai Fujiwara even went so far as to completely eliminate construction details in A-POC ("A Piece of Cloth") Queen (pp. 40–41), a tubular-knit cloth, produced with computer-generated perforations, which could be cut into multiple pieces of a complete ensemble.

In challenging the traditional methods of construction and tailoring, a number of designers de-constructed the fundamentals and laid bare the inner details, which, although components of the unfinished garment, were often as aesthetically interesting as the finished exterior. Such exposure of the tailor's secrets was tantamount to revealing the intimate underwear of the dress; techniques and materials used inside the garment to give shape and substance now became legitimate elements of ornamentation. Interfacing fabrics appeared on the outside. Lapels, buttons, and collars were reassembled and set awry in relation to their traditional placement and function. The lines of wrinkles and creases created patterns on the garment, a role similar to that of lines on a drawing; slashing, tearing, incompatible textures, and frayed edges realigned the sections of a garment's traditional format, making abstraction and asymmetry the dominant criteria of clothing design.

Yohji Yamamoto and Rei Kawakubo promoted muslin, the fabric employed by designers for their "rough drafts," to a textile acceptable for daywear. Kawakubo's soft armor (p. 60), constructed of padded sections deceptively tacked together, refers to the basic materials for shaping as well as the paper pattern pieces of the garment in its infancy. Yamamoto's meticulous stitches writ large, interfacing redefined as fine fabric, and common fasteners reconceived as jewelry (p. 65) demand more than a casual dismissal of these elements as experimental: when hierarchies are destroyed, alternative approaches, new ways of seeing, and aesthetic flexibility must fill the void. Contemporary fashion shares its methodology with the fine arts—making a painting requires the constant

re-evaluation of the whole with each successive brushstroke—and the process itself is integral to the product.

Many of the pieces in this exhibition are by Belgian Martin Margiela, a member of the "Antwerp Six" whose work has been characterized as a paradigm of antifashion, or worse, as a harbinger of fashion's destruction. Instead, Margiela interrogates every aspect of fashion, of clothing construction, even of the very idea of clothing. He collects the fleeting moments of the past and mingles them with moments of the present, reconstructing timeless oxymorons that resist classification and prompt inquiry into the designer's thought process. Exploring the skewed perceptions that come from rejecting uniformity and balance, Margiela may, in a single garment, adhere to traditional construction techniques on one side and abandon them completely on the other (p. 180). Vintage garments are recycled and hand-worked with new ones into unique re-creations, such as his Swimsuit Dress, which incorporates the histories of its varied component parts (p. 100). Interiors and exteriors of garments may be alternatively exposed: nothing is sacred, everything is opportunity.

Like Margiela, other designers are fascinated with ambiguity and transformation. The traditional couturier's finished work of art was inviolate and allowed no intervention; conversely, for many contemporary designers the garment's interaction with the wearer is one of the important elements of creation, and this change of concept is perhaps one of the most significant milestones in fashion's recent history. Examples by Issey Miyake, Takezo Toyoguchi, Domenico Dolce and Stefano Gabbana, Yeohlee Teng, and Hussein Chalayan (pp. 73–77, 80–83) provide, with variations of layers and fastenings, a myriad of choices to determine the way the garment is worn, allowing the wearer to decide, according to moment, mood, and self-perception, how she will interpret the designer's work.

Choices available to designers have increased exponentially in the last decades because of rapidly expanding advances in fiber and textile technology. An unbiased and creative approach to media was also an impetus for inventive use of materials and techniques. An early innovator, Emilio Pucci fused the luxury of brilliantly patterned silk jersey with simple dress design to create multipurpose garments for the modern woman. By exploiting the manifold properties of polyester, Issey Miyake revolutionized the venerable technique of pleating with his 1994 "Pleats Please" collection; a finished garment of polyester constructed two to three times oversize was tightly pleated and heat set in a press. Not only did the smaller, permanently pleated and stretchable garments adapt to a number of body types, they also suggested cubist sculpture—the interaction of pleated planes created an alternative structure, perpetually shifting with motion, but always referring to the body underneath.

Contemporary designers have referenced the past while applying modern methods; others have utilized traditional materials in exaggerated proportions. Miyake and the Japanese textile studio Nuno Corporation brilliantly explored another ancient, yet enduring, medium by continuing the Japanese tradition of incorporating handmade paper into clothing and textiles. Another unexpected use of a commonplace material is seen in the metamorphosis of black nylon stockings into Junya Watanabe's bodice and Gaultier's fluttering skirt (pp. 94–95). The ageless and labor-intensive technique of drawn work is reinterpreted by Watanabe in shredding away the warp on the prominent feature of his denim dress: the "lace" decoration on its bodice (p. 102). Visualizing the garment as a three-dimensional collage, Antonio Marras creates textile mosaics of vintage fabrics and beads. Yohji Yamamoto and Patrick Kelly approach ornamentation from opposite directions: Yamamoto uses only the fabric from the dress itself, elegantly twisted and knotted to form its own decoration (p. 59), whereas Kelly turns regiments of buttons and fake pearls into jeweled trompe l'oeil garments superimposed on the very garments they decorate (p. 108).

Very different aesthetically and structurally than woven fibers, novel textiles with intricate and exquisite surfaces created by designers such as Yoshiki Hishinuma have paved the way for a new generation of innovative design that breaks away from what are considered typical luxury fabrics. Heat and chemical processing have created complex and visually exciting textures that complement or replace beading, embroidery, and other traditional types of ornamentation.

Structural textiles, such as Miyake's pleats and Rei Kawakubo's plasticized paper (p. 118) allowed designers to explore the relationship of the body to its covering, to reconsider the inner and outer dimensions of the body's contour, and to develop volumetric shapes that relinquished their roles as mere envelopes and merged with, or remained independent of, the living armature beneath. With this freedom, designers relished in choices: to idealize the natural form of the female body with miraculously elasticized or clinging textiles, as in the work of Azzedine Alaïa and Hervé Léger; or to expand its territory with geometrical structures such as Miyake's staircase "Zig Zag" dress or his "Minaret" built on successive circles (pp. 131, 163)—like Yamamoto's hoop dress (p. 161), directly quoting the architecturally constructed petticoats from the eighteenth and nineteenth centuries.

The extent to which the proportions of the female form—the size and placement of its traditional demarcations of breasts, waist, hips, and derriere—have played a part in creating or defining the fashionable silhouette has oscillated throughout the history of fashion. Additive structures such as bustles, *paniers*, and cage crinolines maximized, while laced corsets minimized the artificially enhanced body contour. With new textiles and new concepts of construction, designers challenged or mocked the tyranny of the traditional body image, especially the cardinal rule that mandated symmetry of the body's parts. In rethinking the accepted norms of the relationship between body and dress, Rei Kawakubo made clothes with random protrusions, or "bumps" (p. 159). On the woman, the garment was a shape of interacting forms and masses;

Junya Watanabe
For Comme des Garçons
Dress, fall/winter 2002–2003 (detail)

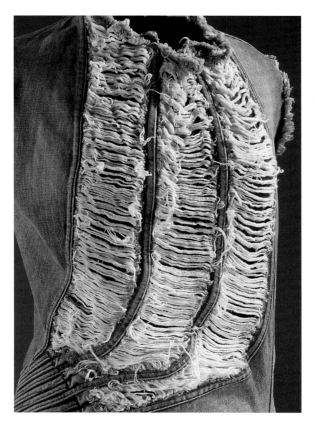

Kawakubo conceived of the dress and body as seamlessly fused into an abstract sculpture.

Kawakubo's quest for a new aesthetic of dress is an example of the focus, for many contemporary designers, on the concept behind fashion design. Many of the objects discussed previously are manifestations of a designer's thoughtful examination of the physical or social environment; many of the objects in this exhibition can be seen on multiple levels because they are so rich in allusions or illusions. Some designers trampled societal taboos about mandatory concealment of certain articles of clothing; risqué underwear became outerwear for Vivienne Westwood, Dolce & Gabbana, and Martin Margiela, who exposed and manipulated the identity of "unmentionables," which are now commonplace in the vocabulary of fashion. Characteristics of the traditionally masculine and feminine versus the ambiguity of androgyny played a significant part in the examination of gender roles expressed through dress, which is illustrated here by Yamamoto's ensemble with trousers engulfed by voluminous yards of lace (p. 187), Gianni Versace's rugged denim shirt paired with skirts of luxurious silk, and Kawakubo's man-tailored suit with embroidered net, which features a wool bra worn on the outside (pp. 188–189, 177).

Costume itself frequently provided inspiration as designers mined rich sources of sartorial function and folly in the history of dress. Christian Lacroix, Thierry Mugler, Gianni Versace, and Gilbert Adrian utilized the panier (a wide-hipped understructure of the eighteenth century named after the French word for "basket"), not only as a model for the architectural form of the garment, but also to experiment with placing a historical silhouette in a modern context. Christopher Bailey, Junya Watanabe, and Martin Margiela deconstructed the classic trench coat developed by Thomas Burberry in 1914 and produced wildly disparate interpretations of this fashion standard. Franco Moschino approached the idea of fashion itself with humor and critique—sometimes subtle, as in his Chanel-style suit with enormous buttons, and sometimes glaringly obvious, as in his "Dinner Jacket" laden with golden flatware, an ironic reference to excessive military ornamentation (pp. 191, 193).

A conceptual approach blurs the line between fashion and the fine arts, and indeed, many contemporary artists use fashion and its sociological ramifications as a core subject in their work. Conceptual artist Andrea Zittel made dresses completely by hand in a variety of materials and techniques as part of her exploration of issues of self-sufficiency—from tools and wardrobes to complete living spaces. Miuccia Prada, Antonio Marras, and Martin Margiela seek to retain the arti-

Franco Moschino
"Dinner Jacket" Ensemble, fall/winter
1989–1990

san's mark by including hand-worked elements in their ready-to-wear lines. Issey Miyake engaged a number of artists for his "Pleats Please Guest Artist Series" to create works in which the dress and its decoration were mutually dependent. With Miyake's "Pleats Please" garments, Yasumasa Morimura, Nobuyoshi Araki, Tim Hawkinson, and Cai Guo-Qiang (pp. 201–205) created ingenious interpretations of a body upon a body: the garment's two-dimensional printed body moving in cadence with, and transformed by, the human body wearing it.

Dynamic changes in the approach to fashion, in construction, materials, form, and concept have created new perceptions about what is worn today: what was radical in the 1980s is now fashion's common parlance. Conventional barriers have been razed, aesthetic demands on designers and the audience have been raised, and ultimately, it is through the reinterpretation, and at times rejection, of fashion's standard vocabulary that contemporary designers have broken and continue breaking the mode.

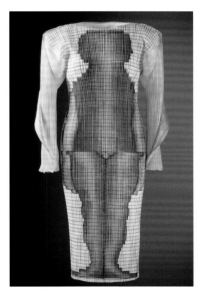

Issey Miyake and Tim Hawkinson
Dress from "Pleats Please Issey Miyake Guest
Artist Series No. 3," 1998

Paola Colaiacomo
Maria Luisa Frisa

Some Random Notes on Italian Fashion
The Fashion of Postmodernism

Breaking the Mode

"Since it's cold and I don't intend to ruin my manicure, I slip on a pair of Armani buckskin gloves. Finally, I put on a black leather trench coat by Gianfranco Ferré, which cost me $4,000."
Bret Easton Ellis

At what point between the two extremes expressed by a garment described, photographed or paraded on the catwalk, and one actually worn, can we place a garment intended to form part of an exhibition? What is its theoretical status once it has been selected to be a part of an "exhibition"? The structure of the real garment is technological: it can be analyzed at the level of matter and of its transformations.

"A stitch is that which has been sewn, a cut, that which has been cut."
Roland Barthes

The real garment leads back to the deeds that have guided its creation: understanding it means measuring, dismembering, and dissecting it, even if only in the mind. Anyone studying fashion is trained to do this. When working with the pupils of the Domus Academy, Gianfranco Ferré once said: ". . . I suggest analyzing clothing through the newest systems, such as computerization and welding, which will one day perhaps replace stitching . . . I want to analyze the problem of designing a garment with precise intentions, by which I decide to design a T-shirt because it is elastic, basic, cheap, etc."

With a slash or a drape, great designers such as Versace or Ferré can demonstrate a constructive detail within a garment, creating a meta-garment that plays with its own evolutionary history, displaying the various phases. Ferré needs only add an extra panel to the front of his Cloud-blouse to reveal the liturgical "intentionality" of the experiment. The silk of the top rests over the organza of the blouse like the stole of the celebrant on the starched cassock for a solemn mass. What emerges are figures buried deep in childhood memories of books: that of Friar Faria in the *Count of Monte Cristo*, for example.

The Curator's Risk

The planning and installing of an exhibition marks an intermediate act lying between the detached approach of interpreting a garment as the interior mark of major ethnic, historical, and semiological systems—and in this sense, the museum is itself a process of interpretation—and the approach of sartorial anatomy adopted by trade operators: like the museum interpretation, it presupposes a contemplative detachment, just as the anatomical inspection requires a preliminary cutting operation. A cut executed not yet on the garment, but through it.

Giorgio Armani ad campaign, fall/winter
1984–1985, photo Aldo Fallai

An exhibition of contemporary fashion has the effect of suddenly illuminating the visitor's own image of himself. We discover ourselves—in terms of "look"—as being born from the destruction of a previous image: we learn that "curator's risk" (M. L. Frisa) lies in taking on the responsibility of bringing about this awareness, which can be painful. Once identified, lifted from a given historical, artistic, and cultural context and inserted in the planned exhibition layout, a style is no longer "innocent." The exhibition intervenes in our daily experience of dressing to go out. In this sense, all exhibitions are of today and about today, and it is in this sense that Richard Martin could speak of the seventeenth century as the incessant century of fashion. If, as in the case of *Breaking the Mode*, the period under consideration is characterized by strong, conflicting innovative currents, the acts of violation the curator must take into account are two: there is the rupture with the tradition followed by the designer, and there is the equally radical gesture of the user who decides to allow himself to be drawn into the rhetoric of new glamour.

"The fashion parade is at Bryant Park . . . Wearing the new models that hark back to the punk/New Wave/Asia meets East Village 1970s, there are Kate Moss with Marky Mark, David Boals with Bernadette Peters, Jason Priestley with Anjanette, Adam Clayton with Naomi Campbell, Kyle MacLachlan with Linda Evangelista . . . However, all eyes will be turned to Chloe so it is all purely rhetorical."
Bret Easton Ellis

Everyday Gestures
He responds to this *Breaking the Mode* challenge by arranging the "pieces" in his mind into four sections: Construction, Materials, Form, Concept. Obviously, this is not a diachronic sequence, but a conceptual paradigm that, applied to Italy, is characterized by a dramatic sense of contrast. The great creativity of Italian fashion in the 1970s onwards lives alongside the radical, conflictual social, political, and economic changes of the country. Traditionally the targets of fashion, women became active and passive subjects in the change in costume, a change that other Western countries had already experienced.

"A feature of the years in which the look that would be favorably accepted around the world from 1975 onwards was still being fine-tuned is the co-existence of two contradictory elements: the extraordinary desire for radical political change and the equally extraordinary attachment to the new prosperity that had been achieved. Italians wanted to be rich, to show they were rich, and at the same time dissociate themselves from the values and social system that had enabled them to become so."
Silvia Giacomoni

It is against the backdrop of these contradictory and continuous changes that Versace's statement needs to be understood: the fashion designer has the power to "revolutionize everyday gestures." In his design are inscribed the gestures, movements, and poses that will render the body visible. Thanks to his special "intuition," the creator dictates the modes of socialization of the figure: adopting a particular style is equivalent to adopting a particular manner of being and of being seen. A "revolutionary" style lives on a revolutionary body. And vice-versa. Promoting this symbiosis means making culture out of the everyday. The power of the fashion designer passes via an infusion of life into an inanimate object.

"Anyone changing the movement of women changes something important. This is what I mean when I speak of everyday culture made by the creator of fashion."
Gianni Versace

Giorgio Armani ad campaign, fall/winter 1980–1981, photo Aldo Fallai. In Maria Luisa Frisa and Stefano Tonchi, *Excess. Fashion and the Underground in the '80s.* Milan: Charta & Fondazione Pitti Discovery, 2004

But in Italy in the 1970s, the movements of women—and, we might add, also of men—were stratified and expressed culturally and socially diversified levels. The cities still expressed their highly diversified history, including that of fashion and ways of dressing. It was from this richness that fashion design learned to gain inspiration.

"In France, fashion is only Paris, but in Italy it is Milan, Florence, and also Rome. It is an integrated process in which every part works together with the others and makes its own contribution to the entire system."
Mario Boselli

Fashion and Elegance
Paradoxically, while the chaotic society of Italy produces a fashion that has wisdom, style, and elegance, an educated, cultured, and efficient society beyond the Alps expresses a fashion that is all brilliance and immoderation. A paradox that the sociologist, Francesco Alberoni, explains thus: "French fashion can be avant-garde and capricious for the precise reason that society is stable there. Creators are asked to experiment, to break the mold; they have to succeed in liberating emotions, stimulating the imagination. In Italy, fashion has not emerged from the avant-garde, but from an ancient and widespread small-scale production system. This system has had to learn how to tackle a modern, disordered, hostile world—how to fight to survive. Italian fashion was not born as spectacle, provocation, or merely as fun, but as industry, to make itself useful, to dress. It did not aim to thrust identity into crisis; it aimed to give it one. And since everybody is overwhelmed nowadays, fearful of the excess and in search of a new rationalization, with its reassuring approach, Italian fashion has scored a bull's-eye."

Gianni Versace ad campaign, fall/winter 1980–1981, photo Francesco Scavullo. In Maria Luisa Frisa and Stefano Tonchi, *Excess. Fashion and the Underground in the '80s.* Milan: Charta & Fondazione Pitti Discovery, 2004

The "Made in Italy" formula as a definition of a quality product in terms of form and content has found one of its most significant expressions in fashion. In the mid-1980s, Milan was internationally recognized as the capital of prêt-à-porter. Krizia, Missoni, Giorgio Armani, Luciano Soprani, GianMarco Venturi, Enrico Coveri, Gianfranco Ferré, Gianni Versace, Moschino, later joined by Romeo Gigli and Dolce & Gabbana, are known throughout the world, not just as creators of clothes, but as masters of style. Each of them offers a clear style that is unmistakable and so totalizing as to be completely identified with its creator.

Then people began discussing "lifestyle." Design made its appearance everywhere. The front covers of *Domus* in those years (edited by Alessandro Mendini) were designed by Occhiomagico and they evoked the new ways of living and of inhabiting concepts in accordance with the exclusive dictates of postmodern design. This postmodern design manifested itself in flesh and blood, dress and music—even at the popular national songfest, the Festival di Sanremo. Matia Bazar, an elegantly cultured band, presented themselves as the snapshot and soundtrack of this trend and won the Critics' Prize for 1985 with their song "Souvenir," made up of elegant electronic melodies.

Flexible Bodies

It is clearly evident to everyone that over the past three decades the expressiveness of women has changed in synch with fashion and that everything is moving toward standardization. The glorious prêt-à-porter of the 1970s had already started to move in this direction, although maintaining a certain decorative sense that was still external to the figure, but which accorded with the grammar of the figure.

"An artist sui generis, an anti-artist artist, always determined to maintain a distance from any label, definition, and limitation in expressive freedom, Moschino shrugged off stereotypes of fashion and art, rebounding between a rupture in linguistic syntax and an evasion of traditional meanings, simultaneously substituting these with a personal reconstruction of images and words. Extraneous to the world of convention and of the predictability of Western myths, this designer of restyling, inventor and re-inventor of new cultural, chromatic, and formal pairing, remains one of the most intellectual figures. At the same time, however, he showed himself averse to intellectualism, active on the fashion scene from the post-war period to the third millennium."
Mariuccia Casadio

With the graphic phase of the prêt-à-porter over, the design of Italian fashion made an ever deeper impression on human anatomy, conforming the body to it. Women had entered social change with a vengeance: in like manner, Mariuccia Mandelli pointed out "the need to consider the entire woman and not merely, as had been the norm before, single skirts or blouses."

It is this thrust toward the "complete woman" that leads to a definitive break with the past. It is this shift away from tradition that "made" Italian fashion so famous around the world today. A world that welcomes it as though it were a figurative gift, one of many appearing through history. But the situation was harder in Italy. The bodies of British women, for example, had already been remodeled by twenty years of independent work, contraception, abortion, and unmarried love. Once started, there was no stopping the pendulum of swinging London; indeed, it had become formalized by a widespread style of urban living. The bodies of Italian women, instead, aimed in this sense to be virgin, or almost, and as such were communicated by the media. And like virgin wax, fashion could restyle them, to excess, resulting in the shameless offering of the almost nude portrayed as the new mass luxury. The lack of resistance those bodies seemed to offer became amplified internationally. The Italian look was the look in a movement that everybody wanted to join at some point or other; from France to the UK and the USA. Different, radically different, was the silhouette that arrived from Japan. What we often forget is that those bodies were so responsive to fashion not out of a simple sense of decoration, but through a wish for ostentation—in elegant terms—of the agitation stirring within them. Fashion declares the depth of bodies that are themselves the artifices of change, at least to the same extent that they are its receptors.

Democratic Fashion

Provocative actions such as burning bras in the streets, the battles fought to wrest control of one's own body, feelings, and time and which required political lucidity and cohesion led to divorce, the liberalization of abortion, anew family condition, equality at work . . . even now. The real and direct knowledge of one's body leads to safer contraception. At the same time,

Missoni ad campaign, fall/winter 1983–1984, drawings Antonio Lopez. In Maria Luisa Frisa and Stefano Tonchi, *Excess. Fashion and the Underground in the '80s*. Milan: Charta & Fondazione Pitti Discovery, 2004

the appearance of small self-awareness groups and consultation offices revealed how what appear to be individual problems are the same as everybody's—a fact that could transform the conquest of a few into common knowledge.

Because, as the theorists of feminism, such as the Lacanian Luce Iragaray write: "The female has no place except within models and laws emanated by male subjects."

"Between a cry and silence, we choose the word," officially declares the Tribunale 8 marzo, founded in Rome in 1979, which aims to give a voice to women and reveal the obvious and not so obvious conditioning that prevents full freedom for women. At the beginning of the 1980s, the image of hysterical, excited, radical women gave way little by little to the image of the new woman, to a different image that the media have helped to spread. Women who have reconciled themselves to men and succeed in their professional lives were soon seen as models. Marisa Bellisario, the first woman to become managing director of a major company (Italtel), was the figurehead: Giorgio Armani outfit, punk hairstyle, firm gaze. A perfect look for the media.

Democratic fashion offered women the means to follow any avenue they chose to explore. Fashion—and not just clothes but also lifestyle—made an explosive entry into how an individual character defined himself, or herself. There was a garment for every type of woman, just as there was a garment for every occasion. While the prime necessity during the day, for work, is to have a uniform communicating calm authority, in the evening and for fun the woman longs to seduce. She wants to taste the pleasure of the hunt. In her bestseller *Fear of Flying*, Erica Jong describes the pleasure of screwing without zips. A dress was sexy in this case, but succeeded in preserving a structure that followed the female form, highlighting it and rendering it autonomous in the eyes of a man. These were garments that did not require a body transformed by gym and plastic surgery, because they had a design, a form that rounded off the silhouette and carved it like an erotic icon and not like the caricature of a femme fatale. Every woman could at last draw up a list of her desires. Awareness and passion at the same time. The pleasure of at last having the chance to consume her desire in equal fashion to a man and to break the rules imposed by male society. Sex was not yet the fundamental element of life, although contemporary society wished to convince itself that this was indeed the case, and so highlighted and then sublimated it in consumption and a patina of marketing. It was still a dark and secret fact that heeded the energy and aggressiveness of nature.

1983: the Miss Italy contest returned after a twelve-year interruption.

In an Italy that was charging ahead, the cult of the image exploded. From a survey conducted by Makno on the theme of the body and seduction, it turned out that 80 percent of Italian men and women considered the physical aspect as being decisive in appraising oneself and others. The period of the triumph of the body, of appearance, of the pleasure in being looked at, had truly arrived. Seduction was no longer just a female thing. And in advertising, the man's body appeared alongside that of the woman. The categories of sex and gender and their respective roles, rigidly identifying what belongs to each group and assigning obligations, duties, and pre-established models of behavior, underwent rule-free assaults from all sides.

A Total Look

The shift from "Made in Italy" to the Italian look forms the major collective episode Silvia Giacomoni writes about: not something "new," not a new look that can theoretically be traced back to an "old" one, but instead an irreversible break with respect to the traditional vision of the female body as a changing and eternally capricious one. If a collector of differences like Calvin Klein could count on women "who buy one thing at a time, without buying into a global look," an architect of the dressed body like Ferré already looked forward to a "basic comprising three blouses, two slacks, and a few skirts." All of which was quite "normal." This was a revolutionary normality, in which the clothes from the last season were not thrown away, but were worth keeping in reserve. More than a stylist, he felt himself the designer of a look.

Since it is a total look, the Italian approach involves the person together with the occasion, the garment with the body, the design with the look, in line with the happy intuition of Emilio Pucci in the 1960s, when he had begun wrapping the female body in light silk links, whose subtle, sumptuous color effects were in themselves enough to "make" the garment. In these thematic studies of single ranges or kaleidoscopic evolutions of entire color hierarchies, there was a specific reference to the clarity of the finest humanist Florentine painting, which had become an "evergreen" style. The human frame had to do nothing other than prepare itself through exercise and visits to the gym in order to absorb so much history and riches: the simple lines and lightness of the materials rendered the garments suitable for all occasions and infinitely versatile. For the increasingly frequent trips away for work or pleasure, only a small suitcase was needed; moreover, what made the difference was the body one carried around, one that was to be well taken care of, agile, reactive. Ready for sports as for society events. Proud to give form to the light silky veil laid over it like a tattoo. The era of the body viewed as garment had already started with Marchese Pucci, just after the war.

Trying to record the specific aspects of Italian fashion in the past three decades is like creating a phenomenology of these "fashioned" bodies, or bodies modeled by fashion. Bodies that bear the imprint of their worldly experience and modeled by designers requiring inventiveness, technical skills, and artisan precision.

"I see increasing need for specialization and creativity in the fashion designer, applied to a pseudo-artisan or mass production, and backed by a constant stimulus toward research. The time for improvisation and spontaneity is over. Rather than a vague, make-do creator, I believe instead in a rigorous, controlled one. I reject half-measures and am against inventions made for their own sake, especially as I believe there is truly little to invent in terms of clothing. On the other hand, the work of the designer has become one of conditioning everything that has been done in terms of new forms. The condition of the clothes designer is that of an individual design that modifies and grows through the manners and possibilities of assembly provided by technology. Underlying all is a personal intuition, and hence the interventions that determine the transformation of original matter, associated with a choice of image or to particular phenomena taking place during the phase of transformation: all depending upon the industrial resources enabling large-scale reproduction."
Gianfranco Ferré

Renaissance Figurative Art

The link with Renaissance figurative art, and through this to the world of antiquity on the one hand, and to the latest results of modern art on the other, is not the exclusive

prerogative of a single aristocratic designer: each of the creators shown here finds his own way to this inherited heritage, and in this sense, the coming of *Breaking the Mode* to Florence was necessary, rather than simply important, since it was in Florence that everything began. Not sixty but six hundred years ago. And just as humanism was, with respect to the centuries preceding it, a total revision and re-invention of all that was human, so the total look Italian fashion has given the male and female figure in recent decades takes its inspiration from the original layers of our figurative culture and injects new elements into it.

"The idea of a power saving and protecting fashion also encloses an invitation to re-evaluate gestures that flatter not only the body but also the soul, according to Marras: hardly any garments by this designer do not require the participation of the person wearing them: embracing oneself in a cape, tying a kimono, buttoning a series of buttons, tightening a skirt with coulisse and tapes, holding back the sacred falls of a cape with one's hand, closing a collar, hooking buttons, wrapping oneself in a shawl. All is soft, fluid, 'surrendering,' but with a single move, it transforms itself into a shield, armor, defense. Strong and fragile, Marras's creatures live their interior nature by transferring it to the garment, in which layers, overlapping layers, applications, and encrustations triumph. The poem Blaise Cendrars dedicated to Sonia Delaunay, who made 'simultaneous garments' using patchwork, comes to mind: 'Sur la robe elle a un corps,' on the dress, she has a body."
Antonio Macinelli

The figuration of the human as it emerges from fifteenth-century Florentine paintings would have been unthinkable without the technical innovations of the period, including those in textile crafts: in the dyeing and preparation of the yarns, for instance.

In Missoni's "chanellini," and in the casually "put-together" look they embody, Arturo Carlo Quintavalle recognizes the traces of the "'innervation' of the culture of textures in our modern society."

In this "textural innervation" there is a great promise of inventive freedom.

"Missoni's vision stimulates me to write."
Anna Piaggi

Armani in *La moda italiana. Dall'antimoda allo stilismo*. Milan: Electa, 1987: *Donna*, March 1981, photo Fabrizio Ferri, model Isabella Rossellini; *Time*, April 5, 1982, photo Bob Krieger; Mural-ad for Emporio Armani, spring/summer 1986, from a photo by Aldo Fallai

But there is also a promise of liberation of movement in the corporeal volumes, through pleasure.

"The success of Missoni is exemplary: his knitwear appeared like a paean to joy in regained freedom of movement; it laughed at the rigidity and formality of jackets and suits, but at high cost, one only the rich could afford. The brilliance of Missoni lay in picking on one element of costume and transforming it into fashion; it is not an isolated fact."
Silvia Giacomoni

Bad Taste
But once the total look has been opted for, there are an infinite number of types: even looking from above, one is struck by the variety of characters of this "woman" who is, more than anything else, a projection of the imagination, a screen on which the desires are glued through the act of looking. Even the conventional rankings of beautiful and ugly are challenged. The effect can even be provoking.

"Since I detest imagining myself in this job, I have avoided the typical choices that make one famous: parades on the catwalk, society events, interview galore. And since I love this job, I have put everything possible into it. A reconciling of opposites that has also guided me in my creative choices. The little backpack that made me famous is nothing more, when all is said and done, than a mixture of industrial materials and attractive trimmings, nylon, and crocodile. On the other hand, I don't like good taste, I don't like beauty. Refinement and taste come easily to me, but it irritates me to surrender to them. When I do, collections come out that are even too popular, like the Chinese one ten years ago, or the very feminine 1940s one. But I'm fonder of my trash soul, because I maintain that, since the 1960s, good taste is dead and buried. I want to analyze the ugly. Artists do it, filmmakers do it; why not a fashion designer, too?"
Miuccia Prada

It is toward this trash direction, rather than a blander one that the revolution of the everyday that Versace speaks of lies. And he speaks of it with great authority, given that nobody has pushed for change—almost violation—in the female form through clothes more radically than himself. He did so without half-measures, in a single move, when he moved the image of the prostitute into the field of fashion design: as visual icon and not, as some pretend to believe at times, as a commonplace sociological affirmation. This point is worth making given the recent furore concerning a hasty journalistic judgment of Italian fashion as "trollop fashion." For streetwalkers or for women walking in streets, which is what fashion is. But in modern Western and Oriental culture, the icon of the prostitute is an all-encompassing one, charged with symbolism and not without authority: from Mary Magdalene to the women of Manet and Renoir and to the pretty woman in the film, via the geishas of Hokusai and the Chinese red lanterns.

The faithfulness to the icon of the prostitute as a major figurative icon saves the creator from the petit-bourgeois humor of facile commiseration or indignation. And he saves his public from misunderstanding that the explicit sexualization of the garment was doable at low cost, without trying. Actually, as is apparent in Chanel also, sex does not appear in fashion without a preparation of the body requiring some suffering: a small daily ascesis. We are reminded of this by the sizing, nurses' safety pins, openings, various breaks and mixings, like those anticipating punks and saris, with which Versace is so prodigious: each of these styles being interpretable as the independent and ambivalent witness of clothing mortification-glorification.

Eveningwear by Gianfranco Ferré, fall/winter collection 1982–1983. Page from *La moda italiana. Dall'antimoda allo stilismo*. Milan: Electa, 1987

The already rich visual pedigree of the Versace prostitute figure takes on a new quality of power, which appears in a radically new context: in the autonomy of work and everyday pleasures. According to the etymology, after all, "to prostitute oneself" means "putting oneself forward": setting oneself up as the object of another's gaze. Understood as right and not as duty, the striving for pleasure provides impetus for the figurative tradition of the female figure. The explosion of graphic and colored insubordination easily noticeable in Versace's style and fabrics cancels the stigma of social and physical inferiority impressed for centuries on the image of the prostitute; this stigma that is one of the main sources of the attraction provoked by the body supporting that image.

Medusa

Versace has printed an ancient and yet "new" mask on the thousand well-known ones of the prostitute: that of Medusa. A good-luck talisman in legend, assigned the position between looking and being looked at, the icon of Medusa translates perfectly into the world of "the look." The cut-off head with snake hairdo, the face that has the power to petrify those who look at it but which is so beautiful it is impossible not to look, is re-interpreted here as a gadget and proposed in brooches, buckles, decorations of all sorts. The logo worked as an intensely figurative jewel, in which the human becomes a hybrid of the animal, and is equally able to communicate the abstract, futuristic "swoosh" of Nike. The horror-fascination that Versace kitsch provokes becomes an instrument of power in the world now dominated by the look as extreme experience: as a neurosis of looking and knowing oneself to be looked at. As though it were a find from an ancient excavation to which it truly belongs, the Medusa head is embraced by Versace and boldly transformed into the symbol of a new, impudent elegance; an elegance of bad taste that barges forward to be admired by all. Rich and poor alike.

Armani

"Women needed a uniform that corresponded to the new mentality they were acquiring."
Ingrid Sischy

It was Armani who designed this uniform, for all of them. In terms of exposure, the task operated by Armani with the female body was an operation that ran counter and parallel to that of Versace. While in the latter, sex is directly power, in Armani it was via power. An approach toward power, but no less decisive for all that.

Outfit by Romeo Gigli, spring/summer collection 1986. Page from *La moda italiana. Dall'antimoda allo stilismo*. Milan: Electa, 1987

Outfit by Krizia, fall/winter collection 1985–1986. Page from *La moda italiana. Dall'antimoda allo stilismo*. Milan: Electa, 1987

Antonio Marras Haute Couture, *Adelasia di Torres (Il Sale)*, fall/winter collection 1998–1999, Galleria Nazionale d'Arte Moderna

This can be already detected from the use of materials: wool, silk, and linen are for Armani compact, for the most part monochromatic, surfaces. Opaque or shiny, they are always extremely flexible because treated to a large number of hard-wearing processes. Beaten, twisted, combed, shaved, the raw material loses the memory of its origins: of the disorder, of the irregularity of its origins, whether vegetable or animal. Made into fabric, the fiber minimizes its own tactile and color impact. The famous neutral palette of "greige" (gray + beige) leaves the room free for the skilled tailoring the fabric must undergo so that the body beneath may receive a form. The material has its revenge in arising anew in an ambiguous silhouette, open to an infinity of interpretations. But always absorbed in the sacred ceremony of the command by which the designer's eye invites us to participate: always on behalf of an imaginary "she."

In Armani as in Versace, the alignment between invention and media time is perfect in this truly twin-like couple of Italian fashion. Thanks to a sort of miracle, the media do not limit themselves to intensifying the consumption of fashionable bodies, but generate them directly themselves, so that the projection of the image takes place in real time and on a global scale. And what is overwhelmed through the chain of imitations and copies is not just the world of celebrities, but the upper, middle, and lower-middle classes. The codified roles of rank and gender thus pass into the background.

The labels are the aesthetic key to the new consumption and, in absence of other, perhaps more certain but difficult to codify elements, they become status symbols. Because the new elegance is aggressive and communicates its significance and cost in direct manner. "Fashion is fashion." And it draws in men and women in equal manner.

"If in the war of the sexes there has been a winner, then that person is Giorgio Armani. For the past twenty years, his clothes reflect the constant changing of society's stance with regard to the sexual identity of men and women. One might even maintain that the designer has literally shaped the very idea of sexuality in the 1980s. Trends come and go, great tailors and designers characterize a moment in time, but perhaps never in the history of fashion has a designer exercised such a stylistic influence over a whole decade with such breadth and depth as did Armani in the 1980s. The power of ambiguity is a strength of which Armani is well aware and, in order to exploit it fully, he does not hesitate to tackle the question of sexual identity, exploring the contemporary sexual paradox using the arms of tailoring."
Richard Buckley

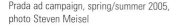

Prada ad campaign, spring/summer 2005, photo Steven Meisel

These extraordinary years also witnessed the male image become more feminine and the female one more male, as well as the emergence of a hitherto denied homosexual identity. The word "androgynous" entered everyday language and acquired a range of meanings. Playing with sexual ambiguity was fashionable, but not only. If a woman in jacket and slacks shifted her erotic charge, it was the man who emerges as sexual object par excellence. And the depiction of the nude male body, in underwear or dressed in clinging clothes, passed from a homosexual iconography to the visual language of the mass media.

Last but not least, in this new iconography, the designer found his own point of representation. He himself became an icon of style.

"The Italian designer shrinks from a way of considering homosexuality in a way that the evolution of customs has rendered ridiculous. But he does not have another working model for the sublime image he wishes to create to hand. So he denies his diversity to the public and limits it within the space allowed by money and power. He fears disdain but cannot hide himself, nor does he wish to. He offers himself in the transfigured image of photographers: beautiful, but above all male."
Silvia Giacomoni

Post Scriptum
We have not intended these notes as captions for images, but as an attempt to restore an ontology of the garment, of its having lived alongside and together with those bodies, those decades that are now over. Of its—the garment's—having made those bodies into the visual expression of a desire and an intention. Desire and intention which for the creators have been defined through the colors and lines they have succeeded in projecting, like so many successive visions, on the surrounding shadows.

The method of construction is a fundamental
component of the design of a building, sculpture,
or garment. Couture-dressmaking construction
techniques of the early to mid-twentieth century
were fundamental to Western fashion; traditional
methodology determined the quality and
appearance of clothes.

Christian Dior's 1947 "New Look" mandated
an hourglass figure with round shoulders, narrow
waist, and voluminous skirts, achieved with
meticulously designed and crafted
understructures. Dior's contemporary, Cristóbal
Balenciaga, instead relied on the substance
and texture of the fabric and his knowledge of
construction techniques to create a garment's
volume and fit. With another vision of the ideal,
Charles James produced complex architectural
monuments of fabric.

In contrast to traditional Western methods of
cutting, padding, and fastidious tailoring to fit
an idealized silhouette, in the 1980s Japanese
designers Rei Kawakubo, Issey Miyake, and Yohji
Yamamoto, in particular, introduced a different
aesthetic based on the Eastern concept of
asymmetry. They used draping and construction
techniques not for perfect fit, but to craft shapes
that were in concert with, or in opposition to,
existing body parts. Issey Miyake has also
invented entirely new methods of construction by
applying computer technology to knitted textiles.
More recently, inner-construction details that
previously were hidden have been exposed as part
of the "finished" garment. Deconstruction and
construction became unified in a functional and
aesthetic goal: both remain vital to the garment's
structural integrity, and both are integral to its
design and decoration.

CONSTRUCTION

Jean Dessès

Two-piece Suit, 1952–1953
Wool patterned twill
Gift of Fay Hammond
M.67.46.2a–b

*Couturier Jean Dessès was known for
his skillful and inventive construction
techniques applied to a range of fabrics.
On this suit, his clever cutting and
tailoring sculpted wide lapels that
disappear into the jacket's waist, and
then create on-seam pockets that extend
into long front panels that are supported
by the A-line skirt.*

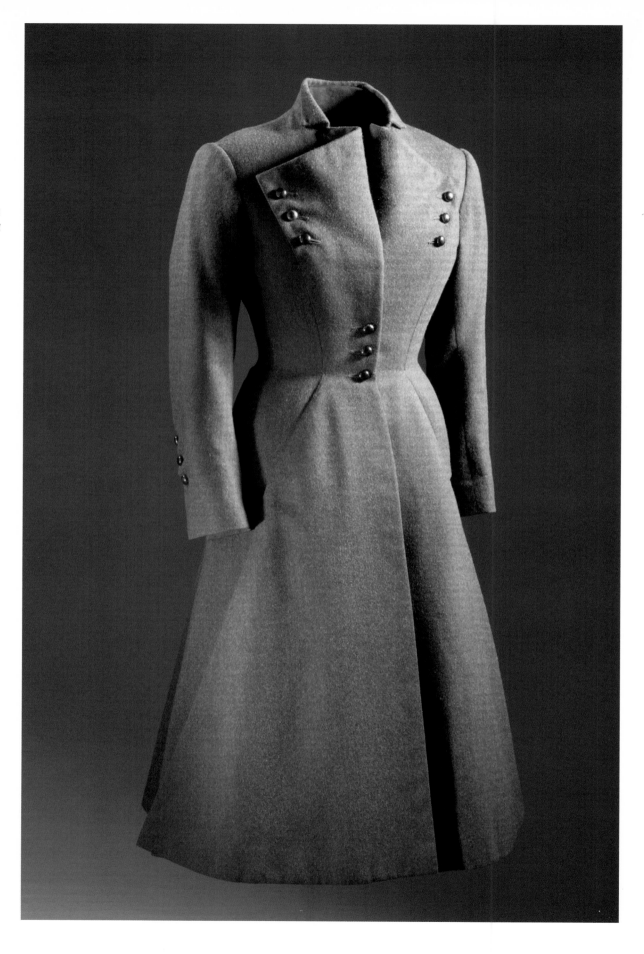

Rudi Gernreich

Dress, c. 1953
Knitted wool
Gift of the Fashion Group, Inc.
M.73.102.6

In reaction to the overly constructed garments of the 1950s, visionary Rudi Gernreich designed this knitted dress ahead of its time. With its inherent elasticity, the garment conformed to the body without boning, padding, cutting, or tailoring.

Rei Kawakubo

For Comme des Garçons
Dress, 1983
Wool jersey knit
Gift of Mary Levkoff in memory
of Akira Kimura
AC1997.152.1

*Rei Kawakubo masked conventional
notions of the shape of the female form
and rejected all dictates of elegance or
finish with a dress that references the
bondage clothing of 1970s punk
antifashion. The strips of wool appear
tattered and torn but are actually
carefully planned and constructed.
The designer's use of black emphasizes
her denunciation of dress as mere
ornamentation for the body.*

Issey Miyake and Dai Fujiwara
For A-POC
Queen, spring/summer 1999
Nylon and cotton knit
Costume Council Fund
M.2002.107.1 (uncut)
M.2002.107.2a–j (cut)

*A-POC (acronym for "A Piece of Cloth")
is an innovative line of clothing
launched in 1997 by Issey Miyake and
Dai Fujiwara. Without using needle and
thread construction, yarn is fed into a
computerized "loom" programmed with
structural patterns. Lengths of flattened
tubular-knit cloth, with perforations
that faintly outline pieces of clothing,
are produced. After purchasing a length
of A-POC Queen, the consumer cuts
along the perforated lines to obtain
multiple form-fitting garments and
accessories. If one tires of the length of
sleeves, hemlines, or socks, a simple
snip with a pair of scissors can refresh
the look—and all without fear of the
fabric raveling.*

Charles James
Evening Gown, 1951
Silk chiffon, silk satin, and nylon
chiffon
Gift of Mrs. Morton Lee
55.75

Jean Paul Gaultier
Blouse and Skirt, fall/winter 1999–2000
Blouse: leather with cotton batting;
Skirt: polyamide nylon and polyester
plain weave with down fill
Gift of Mr. and Mrs. Lee Ambrose
M.2005.139.3 and M.2002.185.1

*Charles James, considered an architect
of dress, was obsessed with the nuances
of his complicated constructed designs.
This gown, with its massive billowing
skirt, is composed of layer upon layer of
silk, boning, horsehair, and crinoline
that formed an armature for an edifice
of diaphanous fabric.*
*Referencing the evening gowns of the
1950s, Jean Paul Gaultier capitalized on
the lightweight, buoyant, and resilient
properties of down-filled polyester,
creating a skirt of maximal volume
without layers of understructure.*
*The blouse, with its exposed back
and harness-like straps alluding to
sexual fetishism, is an idiosyncratic
interpretation of leather for
eveningwear. Gaultier thus examines
conventional notions of elegance in
formal attire.*

Rei Kawakubo
For Comme des Garçons
Evening Dress, fall/winter 1991–1992
Silk taffeta with synthetic fiberfill
and gold lamé trim; hand-painted
with ink and gold pigment
Costume Council Fund
M.2005.112

*Rei Kawakubo substituted the
symmetrical crinoline or stiff petticoat
of the classic 1950s evening gown with
an asymmetrical, fiber-filled skirt.
The wrapping of the bodice with an
obi-like sash, which binds the upper
body without the use of a boned
underbodice or corset, along with the
hand-painted pine tree and padded
hem, refers to the Japanese kimono.*

Christian Dior
Cocktail Dress, fall/winter 1957–1958
Silk faille
Gift of Mrs. Robert Rowan
M.65.39

Jean Paul Gaultier
Dress, spring/summer 2003
Acetate and polyester plain weave
Gift of Lee and Mariana Ambrose
M.2005.140.14

This 1950s black cocktail dress from Christian Dior's last collection is a continuation of his "New Look" silhouette, which was introduced in 1947. The boned underbodice, which dictates the shape of the upper body, was modeled with silk and stitched with darts and gathers. Six layers of rigid net and horsehair form the understructure for the skirt.
The form of this Jean Paul Gaultier dress, like Christian Dior's cocktail dress, relies completely on what is beneath the surface. Gaultier's understructure, however, has a distinctly different purpose. The interior lining, cut slightly larger than the dress and twisted, pulls the exterior in directions that change the silhouette with every movement of the wearer's legs and torso. Far from the perfect, immobile hourglass shape of Dior's, this dress is a piece of kinetic sculpture.

Cristóbal Balenciaga

Cocktail Dress and Cape, c. 1964
Machine-made silk lace and silk pongee
Gift of the estate of Mrs. John Jewett
Garland
M.71.19.4a–b

Cocktail Dress and Coat, 1958–1960
Warp-printed chiné silk taffeta
Gift of Mrs. Frank Fuller
M.59.18.2a–b

Rei Kawakubo
For Comme des Garçons
Dress, c. 2000
Polyester plain weave; printed
Gift of Mr. and Mrs. Lee Ambrose
M.2002.185.24

Cristóbal Balenciaga was a master tailor whose lines and forms were architectural yet designed to flatter a woman's figure. He created elegant structural garments that both caressed and stood away from the body, illustrated here in the contrast between the dress and the coat.
Like Balenciaga, Rei Kawakubo enveloped a woman's body in fabric, leaving plenty of space in which the figure could reside. This dress refers to the 1920s cocoon coat and the traditional caftan as well as to the floral lace patterns popular for eveningwear in the 1950s and 1960s. But unlike any of these antecedents, the shape of this dress can change dramatically according to the way the wearer manipulates the two sets of sleeves.

Alexander McQueen
Dress, fall/winter 2003–2004
Wool fleece and nylon polyamide
spandex with silk satin ribbon
Gift of Mrs. Richard E. Grey
M.2005.208

Junya Watanabe

For Comme des Garçons
Skirt, c. 2001
Cotton plain weave
Gift of Mr. and Mrs. Lee Ambrose
M.2002.185.29

Defying the practical aspects of dress to cover and protect the body, Alexander McQueen created a garment that reveals the body that supports it. Starting with wool, normally used to keep the body warm, he cut away the bodice to a minimum. A built-in bra positions the dress on the body, and the heavy fabric is transformed into a gracefully flowing skirt by the strategic placement of darts and tucks.

Junya Watanabe, with his example of complex construction, imitates the drape of the simple sarong by sewing a rectangular fabric into a curved shape with thirty-one separate darts.

Gilbert Adrian
Two-piece Suit, 1946–1948
Worsted wool twill
Purchased with funds provided by
Eleanor LaVove, Maryon Patricia Lears,
Ricki Ring, and Gustave Tassell
M.2003.95a–b

Lachasse Ltd.
Two-piece Suit, 1954 (detail)
Wool plain weave
Gift of Mrs. Harry Lenart
M.86.396.2a–b

Gilbert Adrian, famous for his classic, square-shouldered suits based on the austere lines of menswear, redefined the concept of ornamentation by carefully cutting, matching, mitering, and stitching together wool fabric. Lachasse Ltd. is recognized for fastidious tailored suits, as reflected in this fitted example. Each panel of the jacket was meticulously cut, pieced, and stitched into place to fit the curves of the ideal 1950s woman's body. The jacket's padded hips accentuate the desired hourglass figure.

John Galliano
Two-piece Suit, fall/winter 1996–1997
Wool twill
Costume Council Fund
AC1996.158.15.1–.2

Alexander McQueen
Two-piece Suit, spring/summer 1999
Wool ribbed plain weave, with nylon
and spandex net
Purchased with funds provided
by Iris Bovee
M.2005.130a–b

*For these suits, John Galliano and
Alexander McQueen looked to the past
for inspiration. Galliano appropriated
the broad shoulders of the 1940s and
fused that design feature with heavily
padded hips for the hourglass shape of
the 1950s. McQueen updated the look
of the 1950s woman's suit with a high-
back collar, wide lapels, a flared but
unpadded hipline, and winglike
sleeves—his own version of shoulder
pads. By placing a transparent panel at
the center of the jacket's back, McQueen
suggested a textural collage of wool,
net, and nude flesh.*

Yohji Yamamoto

Two-piece Suit, fall/winter 2001–2002
Wool gabardine with polyester knit trim
Costume Council Fund
M.2002.65.9a–b

*Yohji Yamamoto challenged us to
reconsider the way construction is used
to accommodate the body and
manipulate its appearance. With this
suit inspired by a sportswear staple,
the tracksuit, the designer outsized the
armhole and shortened the shoulder
seam of one sleeve, overturning the
safety of visual symmetry and creating
a discomfiting visual effect: one
shoulder appears to slope, and the
opposite arm appears shorter. This
disparity is highlighted by just one set
of stripes on the wrapped skirt attached
to the pants.*

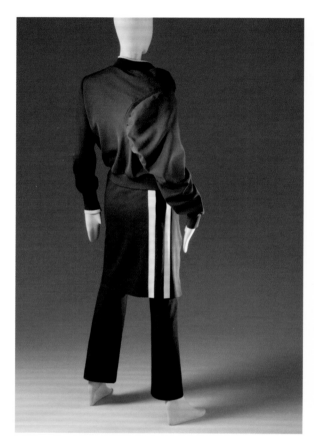

Rei Kawakubo

For Comme des Garçons
Two-piece Suit, fall/winter 1986–1987
Wool, nylon, and polyurethane
twill crepe
Gift of Lee and Mariana Ambrose
M.2005.140.2a–b

*Renouncing the straightforward lines
of the conventional suit, Rei Kawakubo
draped, gathered, and folded wool crepe
back on itself as if it were lightweight
dress fabric. The asymmetrical, soft,
undulating peplum on the jacket is
echoed in the opened seam at the side
of the skirt.*

Yohji Yamamoto

Dress, spring/summer 1998
Rayon and acetate crepe
Gift of Lee and Mariana Ambrose
M.2005.140.10

Dress, spring/summer 1998
Polyester twill crepe
Gift of Lee and Mariana Ambrose
M.2005.140.8

For these two dresses Yohji Yamamoto draped cloth in the direction that it was woven, along the straight grain of the fabric instead of on the bias. His approach may be compared to the respectful treatment given to cloth in the production of the traditional Japanese kimono, which wastes very little fabric and involves minimal cutting and tailoring. The black garment demonstrates a further economy of means: its decoration is ingeniously contrived simply by twisting and knotting the fabric of the dress.

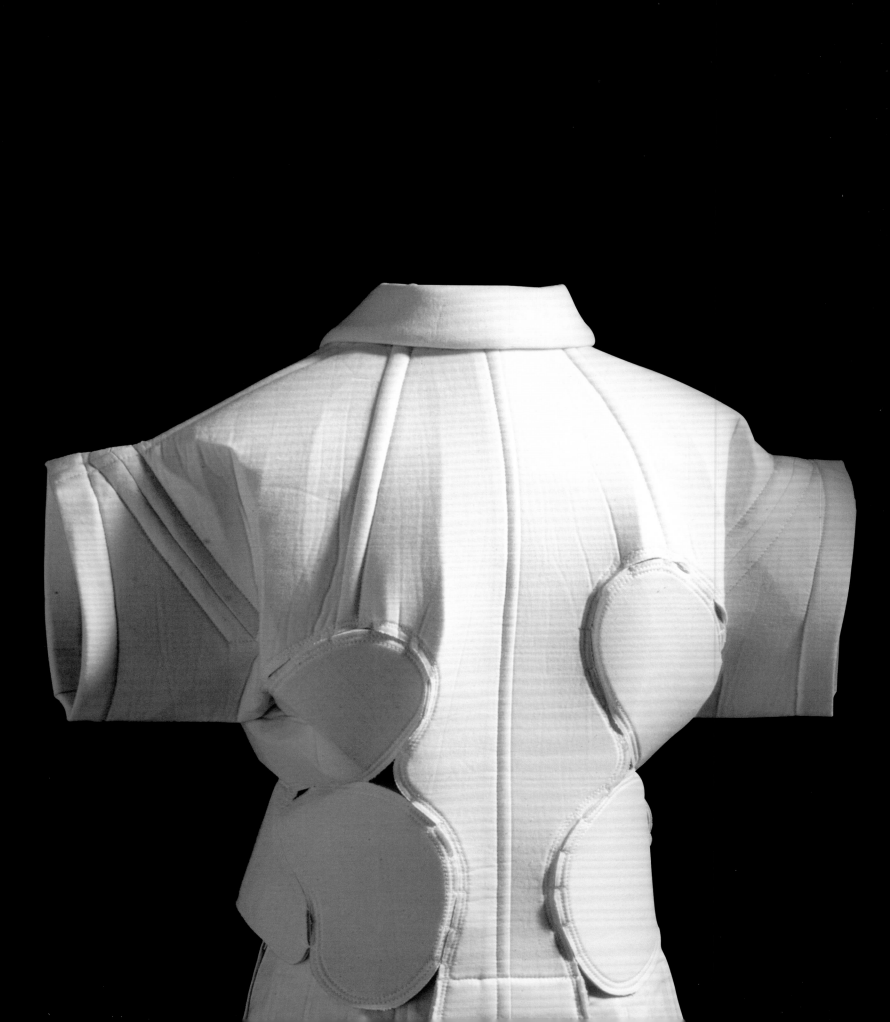

Rei Kawakubo

For Comme des Garçons
Jacket and Skirt, spring/summer 2005
Jacket: cotton plain weave with
polyurethane padding; Skirt: cotton
plain weave with plastic woven tape
boning
Gift of Barbara Fodor
M.2005.87a–b

*Rei Kawakubo used muslin to
emphasize the illusion that this jacket
and skirt are in the pattern stage of
construction. The jacket looks as though
it is made of shaping materials, such
as shoulder pads and suit padding.
And the skirt is formed with woven
plastic boning, another basic
construction material, used to define
shape, curling free-form at the hemline.*

Yohji Yamamoto

Two-piece Dress, spring/summer 2000
Cotton plain weave
Gift of Ricki and Marvin Ring
M.2005.170.7a–b

Here, Yohji Yamamoto elevated the status of undyed cotton muslin, the inexpensive fabric used to mock up a garment prior to production. To further emphasize the association with muslin dress patterns, he used basting stitches as embellishment.

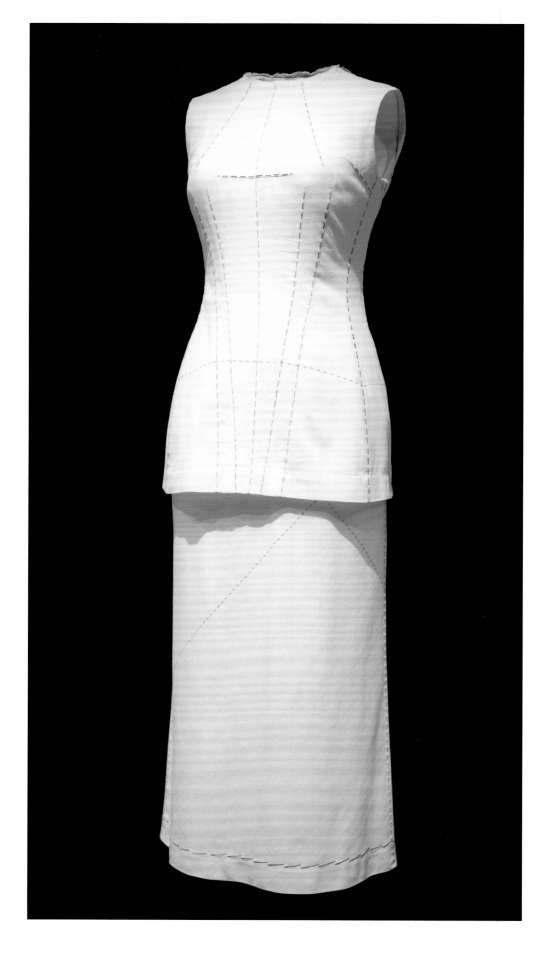

Jean Paul Gaultier
Reversible Jacket from "Femmes
entre-elles" (Women among women)
collection, fall/winter 1989–1990
Silk and rayon twill, wool felt, silk
satin, and polyester plain weave
Anonymous gift
M.2001.164

*The decorative patterning of this jacket
is a map of the complex infrastructure
of a tailored garment: the large zigzag
lines look like the catch-stitching that
holds interfacing in place, and the
jacket's design imitates the segments of
interfacing used to create and maintain
a garment's shape. The interior is the
same jacket, but "finished" with its
structural details hidden from view.*

Martin Margiela

For Maison Martin Margiela
Two-piece Suit, c. 2003
Reversible jacket: polyester and wool
twill, viscose rayon satin, and polished
cotton plain weave; Pants: polyester
and wool twill
Gift of Ricki and Marvin Ring
M.2005.170.1a–b

*On the outside surface of this suit,
Martin Margiela reproduced the creases
that normally occur on the lining.
When the jacket is worn inside-out,
the creases lay flat. The designer also
skewed our perception of perfectly
creased trousers by setting one pant leg
a quarter turn to the right, so that the
stitched creases are on the sides instead
of on the front and back. On the other
leg, the slightly curved front crease
gives the illusion that the wearer is
walking to the right, not straight ahead.*

Yohji Yamamoto
Two-piece Suit, fall/winter 1993–1994
Wool gabardine with wool and goat
hair canvas trim
Gift of Mrs. H. Grant Theis
AC1997.179.1.1–.2

*The tailor's technique is laid bare in
this suit by Yohji Yamamoto. Basting
stitches, which are fundamental to the
construction process, here create an
intricate pattern of surface decoration.
The interfacing, a structural fabric
generally hidden but important to
the final appearance of a well-made
suit, appears on the lapels, where
it is given the treatment of a fine
finishing fabric.*

Yohji Yamamoto
Reversible Skirt, spring/summer 2003
Cotton and polyester twill
Gift of Mrs. Cindy Canzoneri
M.2005.210.7

*Hallmarks of the now commonplace
deconstructed garment are seen in this
skirt's "unfinished" frayed waist,
exposed seams, and the use of structural
stitching to create surface pattern.
When reversed, the white attached
overskirt becomes a structural element
serving as a stiffened petticoat.*

Junya Watanabe
For Comme des Garçons
Jacket, fall/winter 2002–2003
Cotton denim
Gift of Ricki and Marvin Ring
M.2005.170.3

Denim is cut into seemingly odd shapes here, as though the jacket had been haphazardly patched together from recycled blue jeans. The distressed denim and frayed edges reinforce this idea. Undulating shapes that skillfully form a layered shawl collar and flared hem reveal the hand of a masterful designer.

Martin Margiela

For Maison Martin Margiela
"Remodeled" Jacket, fall/winter
2005–2006
Wool flannel, cotton plain weave,
and rayon twill
Purchased with funds provided by
Barbara Fodor
M.2006.34

To make a garment smaller, seams are usually opened and excess fabric taken in. Seams then are restitched, and any excess fabric is trimmed to achieve a smooth, flat surface.

In a radical break from this practice, Martin Margiela's jacket instead is taken in—narrowed and shortened—with extra darts and seams placed idiosyncratically on the sleeves, lapels, and waistline. The excess folds created from the alterations are not removed, remaining instead as a "history" of the alteration process. Thus, the garment is not actually altered, but uniquely "remodeled."

Martin Margiela
For Maison Martin Margiela
Jacket, spring/summer 2004
Linen and cotton twill
Gift of Jan Brilliot
M.2005.141.1

*The deconstruction of this jacket is
an analytical study of how it was made.
The exposed linings, seams, binding,
and raveling threads form the building
blocks of its design. Worn inside-out
or outside-in, the jacket is a perfect
marriage of construction and
deconstruction.*

Martin Margiela
For Maison Martin Margiela
Jacket, fall/winter 2001–2002
Wool plain weave
Gift of Janet Dreisen
M.2005.165.1

*A close look reveals impressions of
a double-breasted jacket with lapels,
pockets, and buttons; however, the
designer compressed an outer layer of
fabric over the jacket front, embossing
the details. The buttons and pockets are
nonfunctional, serving instead as part
of a bas-relief on the textile surface.*

The Interactive Garment

Haute couture was founded on the principle that the designer's concept was paramount and immutable. Throughout the last century, styles have been generated and linked to specific designers, some of whom have been more dictatorial than others in mandating the details and accessories that complete the final look of their creations.

Conversely, some late-twentieth-century designers regard their work as incomplete until worn. Transience and transformation characterize contemporary existence, and fashion, embodying both qualities, is at the vanguard. Not only are pieces in the same collection designed as separates to be selected and assembled by the wearer, but some garments are conceived to be interactive as well. The designer's original idea becomes open to the wearer's interpretation—thus making fashion a vehicle for creative collaboration.

Takezo Toyoguchi
Dress with detachable sleeves, c. 1982
Cotton plain weave with metal snaps
Gift of Rosalind Millstone
AC1997.78.1.1–.4

Takezo's dress, characteristic of the loose and unstructured silhouette introduced by Japanese designers in the 1980s, provides a number of choices to change its configuration. Reminiscent of the wrapping and layering of traditional Japanese dress, the sleeves are detachable, and the wide contour can be modified with a belt tied at the waist or fastened under just one of the skirt's two panels.

Issey Miyake
For Plantation
Dress, mid-1980s
Wool plain weave plaid
Gift in memory of Luna Suyematsu
M.2004.218.8

*At first glance, this shirtdress appears
to be simply oversized. However, upon
closer examination, transformations
of the silhouette evolve with playful
manipulation of cloth appendages.
A rectangular piece of cloth attached to
the waist, for example, can either fall
from the waistline gracefully to create a
short train, or it can be brought forward
around the hips and buttoned to form
an open-front overskirt. Alternatively,
the wearer can place her arms through
slits in the attached rectangular cloth
and drape the fabric over her shoulders
to create a shawl-collar blouson jacket.
Finally, by placing one arm through
a slit, the look of a matching shawl
casually draped over the shoulder
is achieved.*

Domenico Dolce and Stefano Gabbana
For Dolce & Gabbana
Blouse, fall/winter 2003–2004
Cotton plain weave
Gift of Janet Francine Cobert
M.2005.209

*The designers have given the
adventurous wearer unlimited freedom
to play with multiple possibilities in
shape and form; fastening the buttons
in different places makes the blouse
look loosely swathed or tightly
compacted, revealing or concealing—
reflecting the wearer's mood or caprice.*

Franco Moschino

Garment Bag Coat, 1989
Polyester, silk, rayon, metal studs,
and metal hooks
Costume and Textiles Deaccession Fund
M.2005.101.1

*Franco Moschino's idiosyncratic
approach to fashion was
marked by humor, irony, and
incongruity. In an amusing play
on the "multipurpose" garment, his
transformative Garment Bag Coat
is a clever hybrid of a parka or padded
trench coat and a piece of carry-on
luggage. The garment's sheltering
function is doubled; as a coat it protects
the body, and as a bag it protects the
clothes that protect the body.*

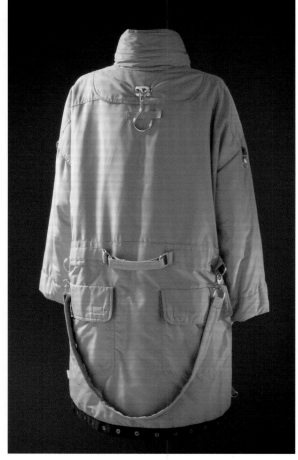

Hussein Chalayan
Two Dresses from the "Medea"
collection, spring/summer 2002
Cotton plain weave with metal zippers
and D-rings
Costume Council Fund
M.2002.223.1 and M.2002.223.2

*Transformation is a recurring theme
in the work of Hussein Chalayan.
This dress, with its companion, is a
garment in transition—a description
in cloth of a mental or physical state.
Its copious ties and zippers, symbols
of constraint and oppression, can be
opened to reveal or tightened to cover
the layers of cloth beneath, or to expose
more or less of the body. The identity
of the dress, like that of the wearer,
is mutable.*

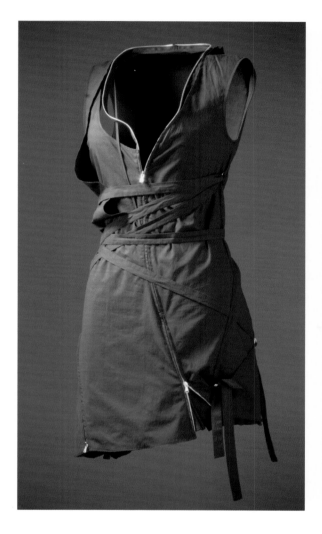

Yeohlee Teng
For YEOHLEE
"Harness" Dress, spring/summer 2007
Teflon-coated Egyptian cotton plain
weave
Gift of YEOHLEE
TR.14979

*A designer whose work is frequently
compared to architecture, Yeohlee
creates maximally functional, yet
strikingly visual clothing for the "urban
nomad." This gown engulfs much space
when its long train is extended, but
for practical purposes, it converts
to half its size when the built-in harness
carries the train over the shoulders.*

Remarkable advancements in textile technology
have altered or diminished the authority of
traditional construction methods. Heat, instead
of labor-intensive hand-pleating techniques,
was used on thermoplastic fibers to create pleats,
gathers, and tucks; new technology thus
encouraged a radical expansion of the vocabulary
of form and the design of the garment as a whole.
Some designers explored new approaches to
traditional methods of construction, reinterpreting
time-honored practices such as lace making.
By featuring synthetic ornamentation, by
combining incongruous materials, or by
integrating traditional materials and practices
with innovative ideas, designers assaulted
conventional notions of luxury and elegance.
The dictates of what was "suitable" or
"appropriate" were sabotaged.
New textiles for fashion and interiors include
three-dimensional structures designed by
computer with sculpted surfaces that replace the
traditional techniques of embroidery and beading.
Topographical surfaces are achieved with such
processes as chemical blistering, spatters and
laminates of metallic particles, heat molding and
treating, and various complex novelty weaves.
With rapidly evolving technology, the potential for
textile development will continue to change the
look and perception of fashion.

MATERIALS

Madame (Alix) Grès

Evening Dress, 1961
Silk jersey knit
Gift of I. Magnin & Co.
M.63.10.3

Madame Grès, who was known for her elegantly pleated eveningwear, started this dress with a stiff, boned inner-corset with wired bust pads. Over this structure she hand-pleated and stitched endless yards of silk jersey across the bodice, then let the fabric fall freely from the waist. Her gowns echo the look of classical marble statues.

Rosita and Ottavio Missoni
Two-piece Dress, spring/summer 1973
Rayon knit
Gift of Missoni
TR.15002a–c

*Capitalizing on the interplay of color
and form created by pleats in fluid
motion, the designers produced a
distinctive style based on complex
geometric patterns in brilliant or subtle
color combinations, thus putting an end
to knitwear's conservative, utilitarian
image.*

Mariano Fortuny

"Delphos" Dress, late 1920s
Silk plain weave with Venetian glass
beads and silk cord trim; stenciled silk
satin belt
Gift of Mrs. Barbara Poe
CR.70.6a–b

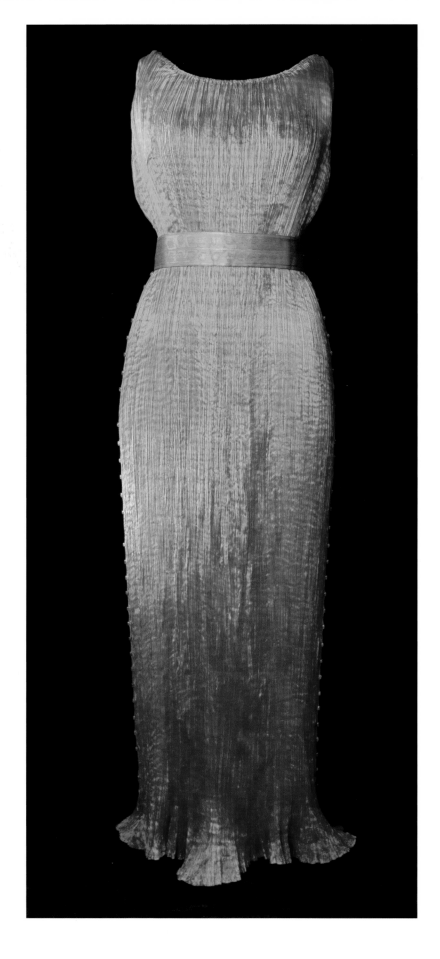

Issey Miyake and Tim Hawkinson
Dress from "Pleats Please Issey Miyake
Guest Artist Series No. 3," 1998
Polyester knit; printed and pleated
and heat- and pressure-set
Gift of Dale and Jonathan Gluckman
AC1999.99.2

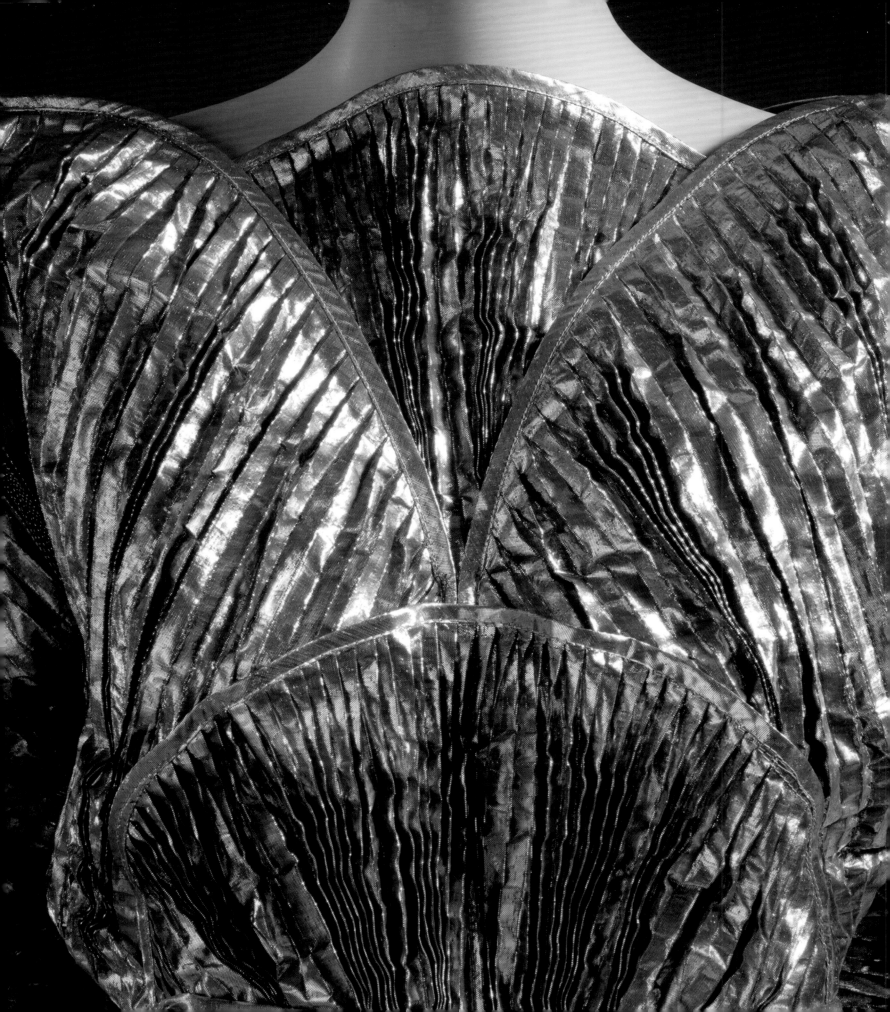

Mariuccia Mandelli

For Krizia
Suit inspired by the decorative arches
atop the Chrysler Building, 1983
Suit: silver metallic cellulose acetate,
pleated; Belt: leather and metal
Gift of Krizia
TR.15010.1a–b

Dress, 1983
Dress: silver metallic cellulose acetate,
pleated; Belt: polyester plain weave
Gift of Krizia
TR.15010.2a–b

Reminiscent of the chiton, *the basic
women's garment of ancient Greece,
Mariano Fortuny's "Delphos" dress was
made by the renowned method of
pleating he patented in 1909.
Contemporary designers Krizia and
Issey Miyake have both investigated
the abundant potential for innovation
in the ancient process of pleating.
The technique can be used to make a
textile rigid; Krizia's jumpsuit, inspired
by a building, expands the body's
presence architecturally. Conversely, the
capacity of pleats to softly define the
figure's contour is well demonstrated
by Miyake's dress with Tim Hawkinson's
transferred drawing of a body that
narrows or widens according to the size
of the wearer.*

Issey Miyake
"Tidal Wave" Dress, 1993
Polyester plain weave; pleated
and heat- and pressure-set
Gift in memory of Luna Suyematsu
M.2004.218.12

Sewn from two identical oversized
shaped pieces of cloth, this dress was
gathered up horizontally and placed
into a heated press to permanently set
the pleats. Once released and allowed to
hang both on and away from the body,
the voluminous yet lightweight dress
bounces freely with every step.

Issey Miyake
Two-piece Pantsuit from the "Pleated
Wave" series, fall/winter 1993–1994
Polyester plain weave; pleated
and heat- and pressure-set
Costume Council Fund
AC1996.158.2.1–.2

*Issey Miyake's signature narrow vertical
pleating is combined with wide rounded
horizontal pleats that create convex
and concave impressions reminiscent
of shimmering water waves or ripples.*

Junya Watanabe
For Comme des Garçons
Blouse, spring/summer 2006
Nylon and polyester knit stockings
Gift of Grace Tsao
M.2006.69.3

Jean Paul Gaultier
Skirt, spring/summer 2002
Rayon knit stockings
Costume Council Fund
M.2002.223.3a

*Both this blouse, by Junya Watanabe,
and skirt, by Jean Paul Gaultier, explore
the idea of transformation by
manipulating one form of clothing to
create another, thereby challenging
conventional ideas about ornamentation
and the appropriate use of materials.
These garments are made of stockings
sewn diagonally around the body;
fluttering stocking feet create an
innovative interpretation of fringe.*

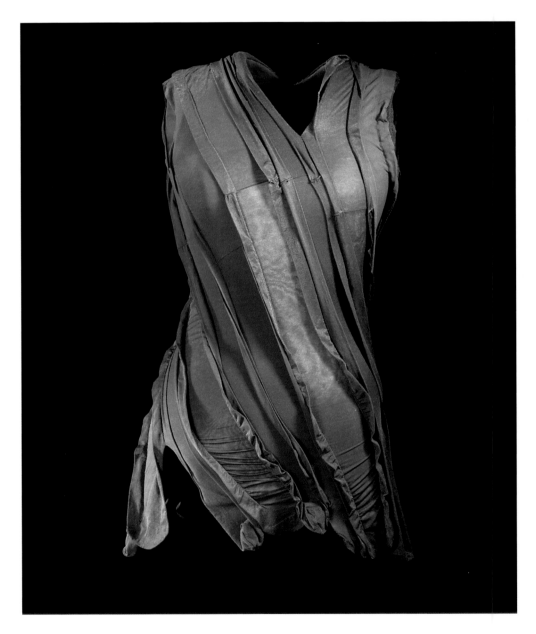

Emilio Pucci
Dress, 1970
Printed silk jersey
Gift of Cindy and Anthony Canzoneri
AC1997.195.1

Cape, 1969
Cotton terry cloth
Gift of Mrs. Craig Castilla
M.2004.30.1

*Complex, colorful, and extraordinary
textile designs complemented by
simplicity in style and construction of
the garment made the work of Emilio
Pucci extremely distinctive. Disdaining
the artificially constructed, idealized
feminine silhouette of Parisian haute
couture in the 1950s, he created instead
clothing for the contemporary woman
of the 1960s—active, professional,
confident, and elegant.*
*A forerunner of a number of post-1980s
designers, Pucci's visionary clothes were
unique in their syncretism. In his
innovative fusion of high fashion and
sportswear, the brilliantly saturated
colors and complex linear landscapes
of his textiles made a single garment
suitable for many occasions,
appropriate for day or for evening wear.*

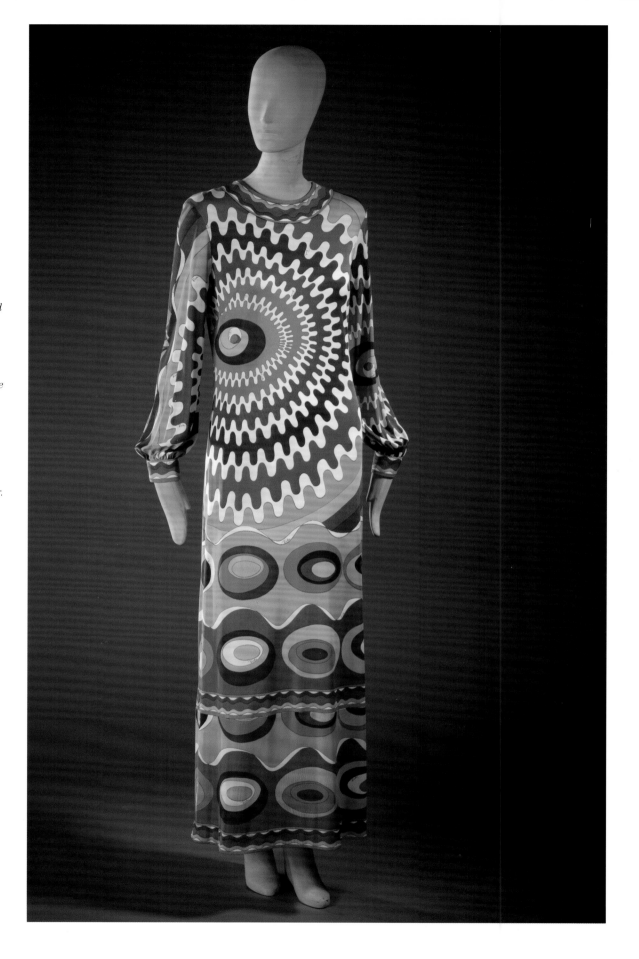

Issey Miyake
Short Coat, 1985
Handmade mulberry fiber paper
Gift of Jo Ann and Julian Ganz Jr.
AC1995.180.1

For centuries the Japanese have made paper and used it for woven-paper textiles, as inner linings for capes, and for constructed paper kimonos. Issey Miyake perpetuated this tradition with his short coat made of large sheets of handmade paper. He also used oil-treated handmade paper to create water-resistant coats worn during Japan's spring showers and summer typhoons.

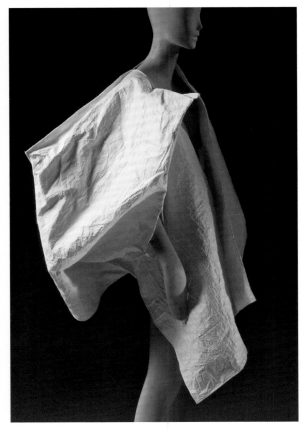

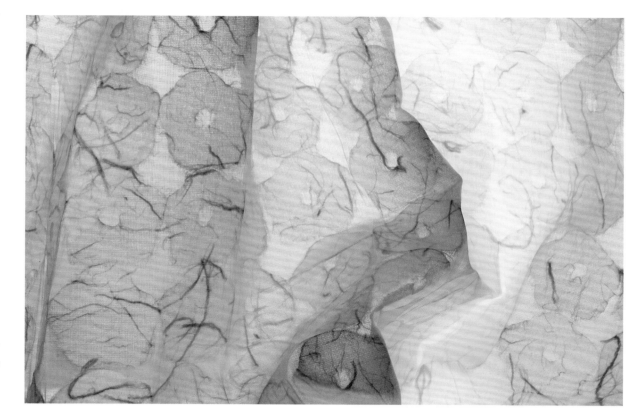

Reiko Sudo
For Nuno Corporation
Textile Length, "Paper Cookie," 2003
Handmade paper on ramie plain weave
Gift of Grace Tsao
M.2006.151.3

A repeat pattern of circles, based on the shape of a well-known cookie produced in Kyoto, Japan, is cut from large sheets of handmade paper and applied to ramie fabric.

Reiko Sudo
For Nuno Corporation
Textile Length, "Yaburegami (Patched Paper)," 1997
Handmade-paper supplementary weft patterning on polyester plain weave; hand-cut
Gift of Grace Tsao
M.2006.151.5

Narrow strips of handmade paper were woven intermittently into this textile. The floating, exposed paper threads were then carefully hand-cut to create the finished texture.

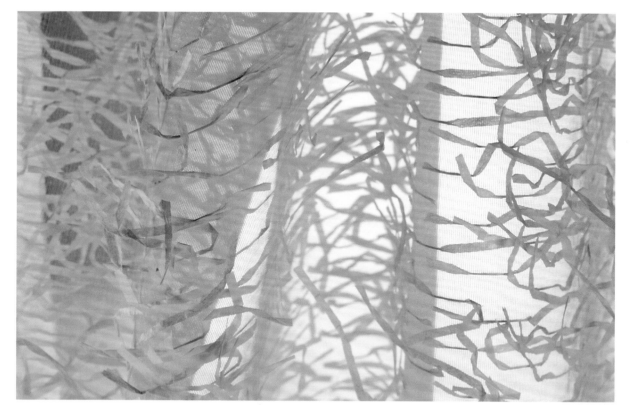

Martin Margiela
For Maison Martin Margiela
Dress, fall/winter 2001–2002
Polyester knit swimsuits
Gift of Rini Kraus
M.2005.168

Antonio Marras
Ensemble, "Eleonora d'Arborea,"
fall/winter 2003–2004
Jacket: silk, polyester, felt, sequins,
and beads; Skirt: cotton eyelet, lace,
faille, polyester, sequins, and beads;
Hat: wool felt; Hat Ornaments: coral
Gift of Antonio and Patrizia Marras
TR.15003a–f

*Recycling vintage fabrics or garments
is an essential element of Martin
Margiela's design philosophy. In this
example from his hand-worked,
or "artisanal" garments, the designer
fashioned new and vintage bathing suits
into a complex mosaic of seams and
patterns.*
*Antonio Marras assembles impressive
conglomerates of creatively altered
vintage textiles, individually adapted
and patterned with stitching and
embroidery.*

Junya Watanabe

For Comme des Garçons
Dress, fall/winter 2002–2003
Cotton denim
Gift of Ricki and Marvin Ring
M.2005.170.2

*Many contemporary designers produce
fascinating results by experimenting
with time-honored practices. Lace, an
openwork technique used for centuries,
is suggested in this garment's
threadbare, latticed effect, which is
created by selectively removing the
textile's warps.*

Domenico Dolce and Stefano Gabbana
For Dolce & Gabbana
Dress and Shawl, fall/winter 1993–1994
Silk chiffon, acetate
Gift of Marianna Ambrose
AC1998.195.9.1-.2

Domenico Dolce and Stefano Gabbana allude to the mythic and romantic visions of Sicily that are evoked by the long rippling fringe of vintage shawls. The shawl serves not only as an inspiration for this dress, but also as its underskirt, wrapped by voluminous swags of silk chiffon in the designers' signature black and white.

103

Akihiko Izukura

Textile Length for "Karakumi Dress"
from the Signature Collection, 2005
Silk ribbon plain weave; braided
Purchased with funds provided
by Carol Mancino
M.2006.14

"Karakumi Dress" from the Signature
Collection, 2005
Silk ribbon plain weave; braided
Purchased with funds provided by
Jacqueline Burdorf and Linda Freund
M.2006.15

Akihiko Izukura's "Karakumi Dress"
is composed of narrow silk ribbons
manipulated on a special loom that can
produce a single length of cloth, both
woven and braided. The textile length
is then folded in half and stitched along
the sides to create an elegant sheath
dress. The seamless transition from
the braided bodice to the dress's woven
body was further enhanced by
the subtle color transition between
the persimmon-dyed bodice and the
indigo-dyed body.

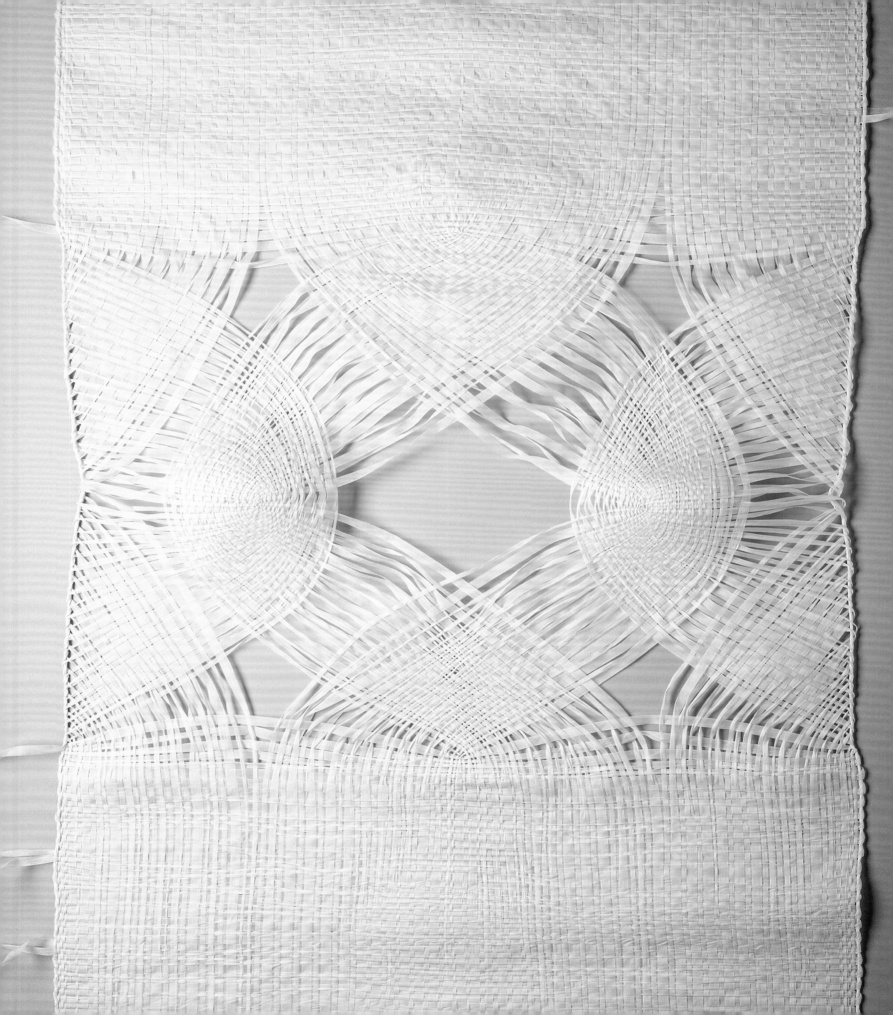

Thierry Mugler

Two-piece Suit, c. 1985
Silk velvet trimmed with rhinestones,
glass sequin beads, and diamanté
buttons
Costume Council Fund
M.2005.106a–b

*Glamour and historical references are
hallmarks of Thierry Mugler's work, as
is a fascination with the aesthetic value
of extreme proportions. This suit was
derived from the mode of the
"incroyable" (unbelievable), the term
for an eighteenth-century French male
fashion extremist who earned the name
by affecting an exaggerated masculine
style based on English costume.
That silhouette, with its extremely high
collar, magnified lapels, and snug-fitted
waist, was recaptured in this
contemporary woman's suit.*

Thierry Mugler

"Anatomique Computer" Two-piece
Suit, fall/winter 1990–1991
Rayon/cotton velveteen with plastic
cord trim
Costume and Textiles Special Purpose
Fund
AC1997.278.2.1–.2

*Thierry Mugler's "Anatomique
Computer" suit represents a computer
rendering of the human body in three
dimensions. Its creation, however,
required significant human
participation: each chartreuse plastic
cord line was individually set and
painstakingly stitched into place with
a clear nylon filament.*

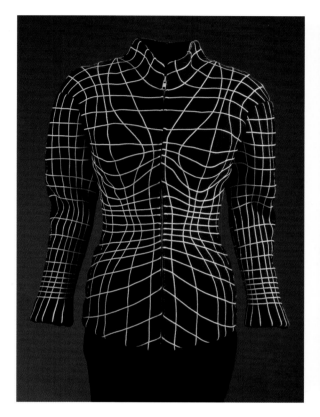
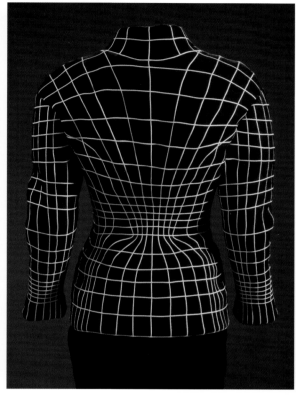

Patrick Kelly

Dress, c. 1989
Wool knit with metal button trim
Gift of Margo Winkler
AC1997.135.10

Dress, c. 1989
Wool knit with faux pearl trim
Gift of Margo Winkler
AC1997.135.9

Materials can be invested with meaning beyond their original purpose. For Patrick Kelly, the use of miscellaneous trimmings (buttons in particular) as the garment's primary focus was loaded with charged memory of his upbringing in Mississippi. As a child, his grandmother repaired his clothes with mismatched buttons. Kelly identified this aesthetic with a kind of empowered ownership of his boyhood poverty and applied it to high fashion.

Rei Kawakubo
For Comme des Garçons
Dress, spring/summer 2001
Cotton plain weave, cotton canvas,
and polyester sheer crepe; printed
Gift of Ricki and Marvin Ring
M.2005.170.8

Rei Kawakubo plays on the meaning of
camouflage in this dress with draped
overlays of sheer cloth that partially
obscure the patterns beneath. Usually
hidden from view in a conventionally
tailored garment, the seams and frayed
edges here are exposed. Soft draping on
the dress creates a dynamic contrast to
the austere construction of the military
uniforms that inspired it.

Miuccia Prada

For Prada
Coat and Skirt, fall/winter 2007–2008
Coat: silk weft-faced twill, felted
mohair, polyester paillettes, and
feathers; Skirt: coated mohair knit;
Socks: silk knit
Gift of Prada
TR.15008a–d

*Unfettered by preconceived ideas about
"appropriate" materials and techniques,
Miuccia Prada combined markedly
disparate textures on this coat: from
fuzzy mohair to woven silk that
resembles Persian lamb fur, to fluttering
plastic strips that imitate the feathers
they surround.*

Norma Kamali
For OMO
Two-piece Ensemble, 1988
Synthetic fur
Gift of Gale Hayman
M.2004.252.5a–c

Plush, a form of simulated fur, has been used for centuries. Advancements in polymer technology gave synthetic fur a more realistic appearance, which, along with responding to the pleas of animal activists, prompted designers to make it part of the fashion vernacular.

Yoshiki Hishinuma
Coat, fall/winter 1997–1998
Polyester plain weave; laminated
with urethane
Gift of Mr. and Mrs. Lee Ambrose
M.2002.185.10

After this coat was constructed,
urethane was laminated onto
the surface of its double-layered fabric,
and simultaneously, a grid pattern
was imprinted using heat and pressure.
The end result is a coat that falsely
looks as though it were made from
reptilian skin or quilted leather.

Yoshiki Hishinuma
Two-piece Suit, fall/winter 1997–1998
Polyurethane and nylon
Gift of Mr. and Mrs. Lee Ambrose
M.2002.185.11a–b

Smocking, the decorative needlework
associated with gathered details
on infants' and children's clothing,
is applied unexpectedly to the thick
synthetic leather of this adult suit.
The result transforms the tough image
of black leather clothing to an
ultrafeminine look.

113

Reiko Sudo
For Nuno Corporation
Textile Length, "Lath Screen," 2004
Nylon josette and wool felt
Gift of Susanna Mercedes
M.2006.150.7

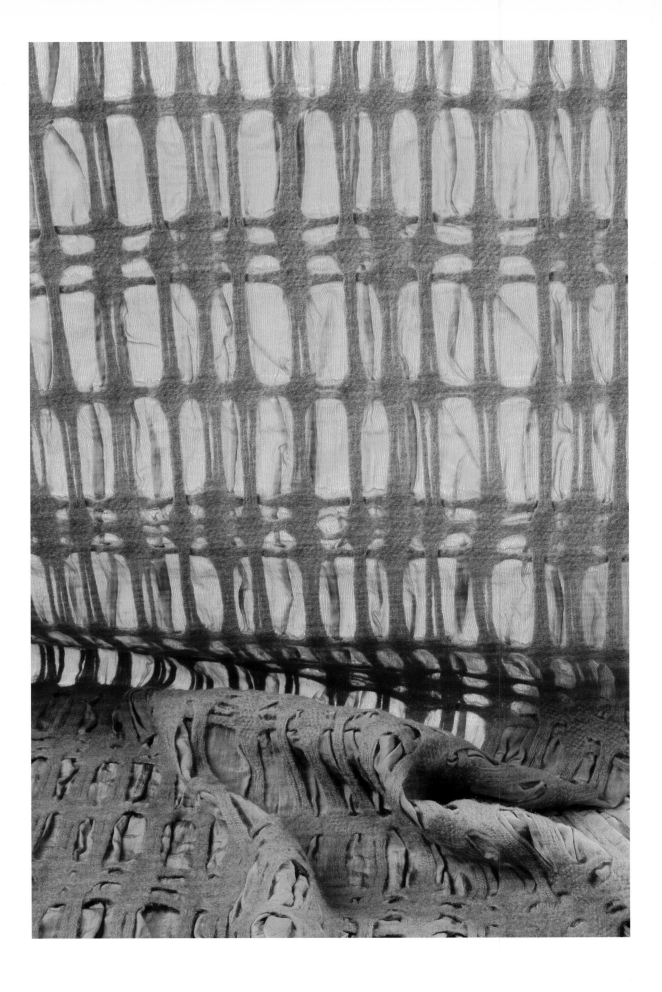

Reiko Sudo
For Nuno Corporation
"Origami Pleats," 1997
Polyester plain weave; heat-set folds
and transfer printed
Gift of Grace Tsao
M.2006.151.8

Reiko Sudo
For Nuno Corporation
Textile Fragment, "Karadaki
(Burner Dye)," 2000
Stainless steel fiber and cotton plain
weave; hand-torched
Gift of Susana Mercedes
M.2006.150.1

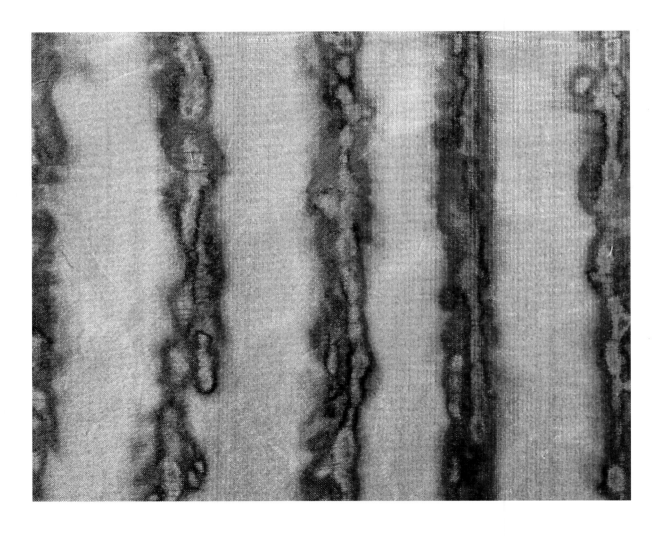

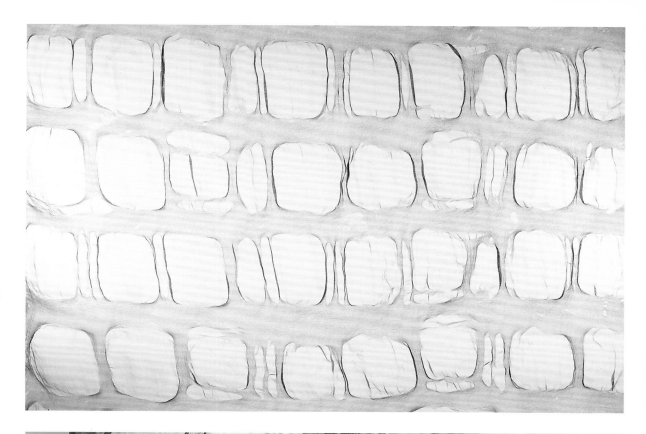

Reiko Sudo

For Nuno Corporation
Textile Length, "Stratus" from the
"Cloud" series, 1992
Silk organdy; hand-applied starch-resist
and salt-shrink process
Gift of Grace Tsao
M.2006.151.4

After a starch paste was hand-painted onto dyed silk organdy in a repeating pattern of squares, the fabric was immersed in a sodium sulfate solution, causing the exposed areas of cloth to shrink. When the starch-paste resist was washed away, a beautiful textural pattern emerged.

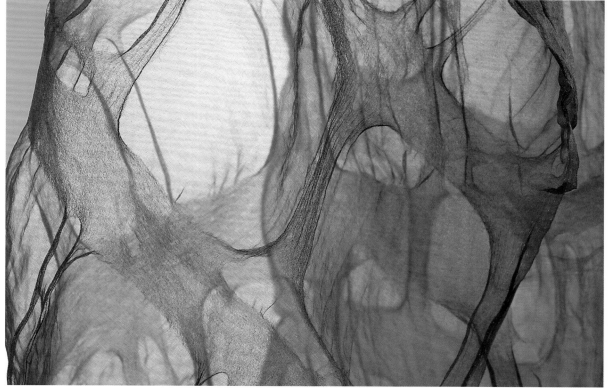

Rei Kawakubo

For Comme des Garçons
Cape, spring/summer 1997
Polyester organdy; gathered, stitched,
and heat- and pressure-set
Gift of Mr. and Mrs. Lee Ambrose
M.2002.185.25

Skirt, spring/summer 1997
Machine-made paper with woven
plastic backing
Gift of Caroline Schwarcz
AC1997.155.1.2

*Building on the historical use of paper
in both Western fancy dress and as
interfacing material, Rei Kawakubo
utilized paper backed with plastic
in this variation of the bubble skirt,
but one with an asymmetrical hem
and a contour that changes with
manipulation. The cape material is
gathered, stitched, and heat-pressed to
create texture and self-ornamentation.*

Issey Miyake
"Pao" Coat, spring/summer 1995
Polyester plain weave; appliquéd
and pleated and heat- and pressure-set
Gift of Mrs. Cindy Canzoneri
M.2005.210.1

A collage of bright bold shapes of fabric
was sandwiched between transparent
polyester fabric, creating a composition
similar to that of colorful abstract
painting. Then the coat was folded
strategically and put through a heated
press to create horizontal pleats.
The pleated polyester stands away
from the body, achieving a sharp,
angular silhouette.

Yoshiki Hishinuma
Scarves, spring/summer 1997
Polyester plain weave and polyurethane;
transfer printed and pleated and heat-
and pressure-set
Gift of Mr. and Mrs. Lee Ambrose
M.2002.185.15, M.2005.140.34–35

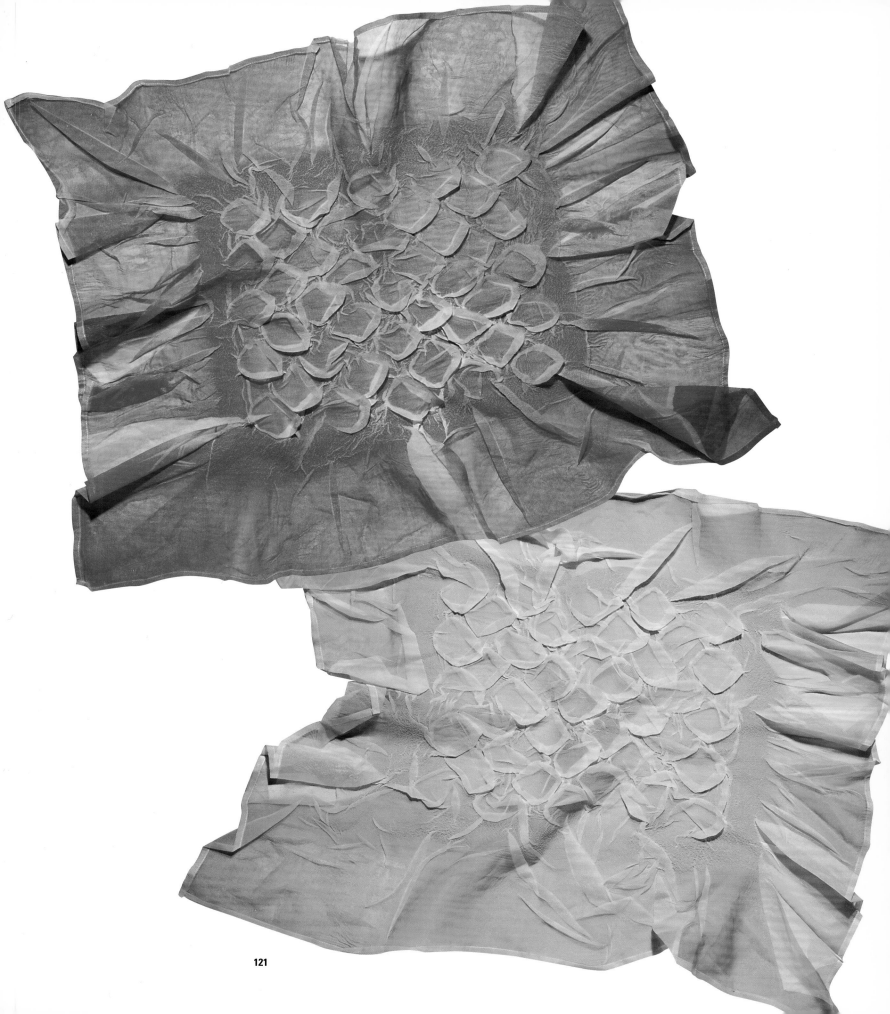

Issey Miyake
Scarf, 1989
Silk organza; clamp-resist dyed and
pleated and heat- and pressure-set
Gift of Bernard Kester
AC1995.72.1

Here, two squares of silk organza were
each folded in half, stitched together,
and folded again. Then, on a quarter
turn, the folded squares were
sandwiched between two pieces
of grooved wood. Next, a dark-brown

dye was poured through the grooves,
coloring any exposed silk and creating
a striped pattern when released. Finally,
the folded silk was placed into a heated
pleating press for its final shaping.

Salvatore Ferragamo

"Invisible" Sandal, 1947
Sueded leather, leather, and nylon thread
Gift of Salvatore Ferragamo, Inc.
AC1992.246.1

Salvatore Ferragamo was the first shoe designer to effect the marriage of comfort and artistic fantasy in fashion's most essential accessory, making the shoe a focal point of creative design, imaginative use of materials, and innovative construction techniques. First achieving fame as the "shoemaker to the stars" in Hollywood, Ferragamo continued his career in Florence, producing remarkable experiments that forever changed the conventional concept of footwear and its role in fashion.

Pair of Split-toe Boots (*Jikatabi*)
Japan, c. 2005
Cotton twill, leather, rubber, metal tabs,
and cotton cord
Anonymous gift
M.2006.70a–b

Martin Margiela
For Maison Martin Margiela
Pair of "Tabi" Boots, 2005
Leather
Gift of Sally Kroener
M.2005.189a–b

Pair of "Tabi" Boots, c. 2003
Patent leather, metal tabs, and cotton
cord
Gift of Ms. Rena Jacobs
M.2005.167.2a–b

*Martin Margiela's signature "Tabi" boot
is inspired by the traditional Japanese
divided-toe padded sock (tabi) which
fastens with metal tabs. In the
nineteenth century, the sock was
combined with the rubber sole of
a Western-style boot to produce flexible
footwear (jikatabi) for construction
and agricultural workers. Margiela's
fashionable "Tabi" boots, always
created from fine leather, patent leather,
or velvet, and sometimes hand-painted,
are quite the opposite of traditional
Japanese boots both in materials and
function.*

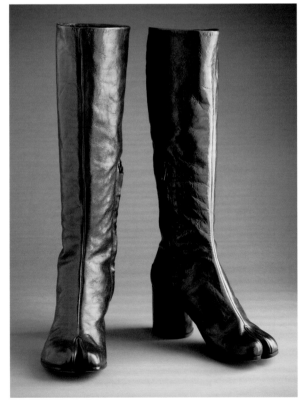

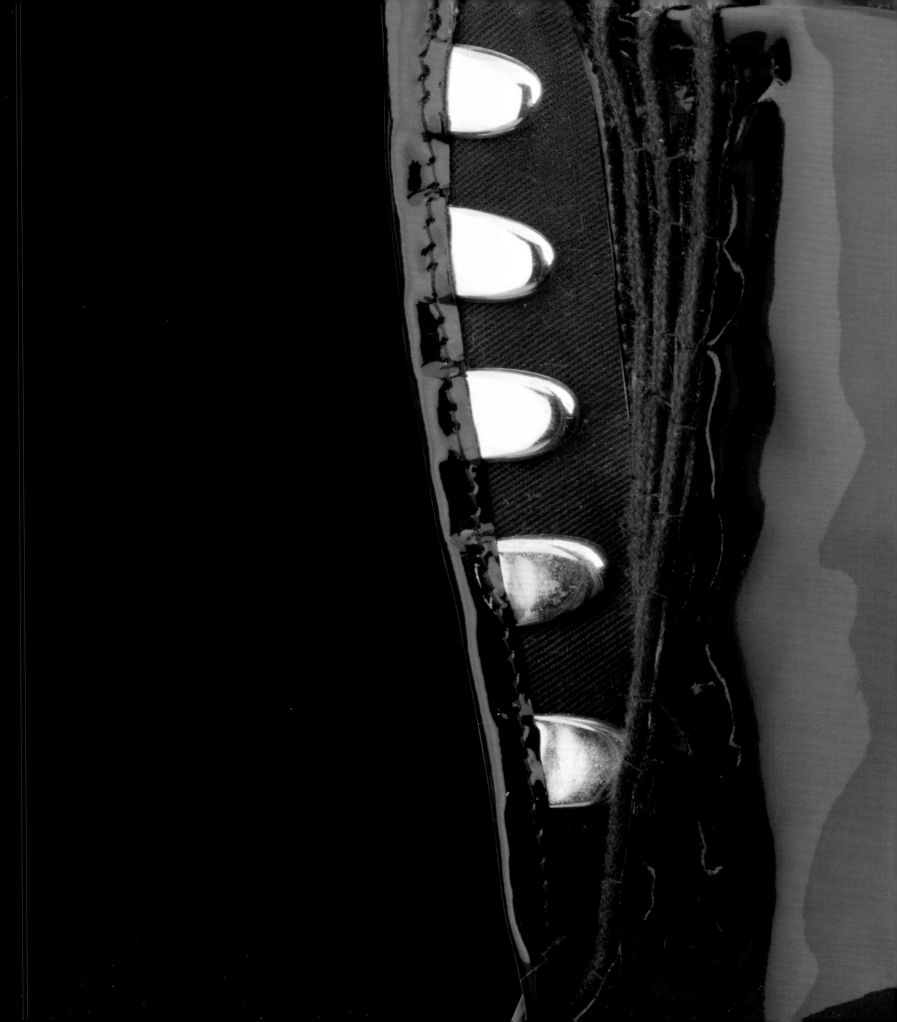

Philip Treacy
"Miracle" Hat, spring/summer 1993
Stiffened machine-made lace, jet beads,
and wire
Costume Council Fund
AC1996.158.18

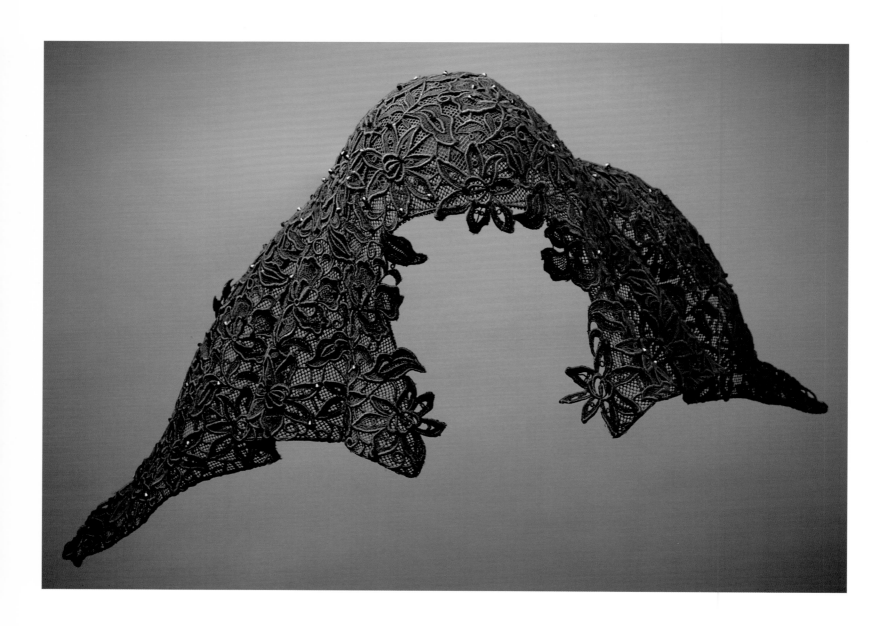

Philip Treacy
Hat, 2000
Silk net and wire
Gift of Mr. and Mrs. Lee Ambrose
M.2002.185.41

The once required hat evolved into an opportunity for designer and wearer to *disregard the practical concerns of sheltering/shading/protecting the head. Whether through use of proportion, material, or understructure, these designs of modern millinery defy the practical conventions of their predecessors and function alone as works of sculpture.*

Yohji Yamamoto
Hat, 1988
Braided straw and wire
Gift of Mariana Ambrose
AC1998.195.11

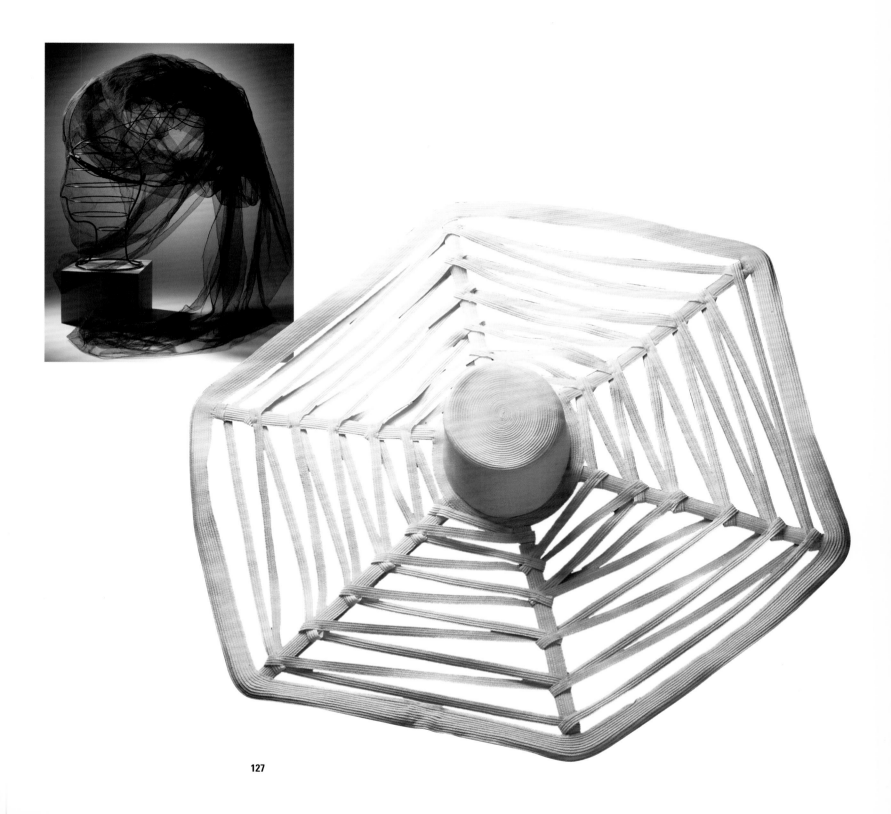

History has borne witness to the oscillating extremes of fashion relating to the parts of the human body. Focus on, and consideration of, the torso and its component parts—bust, waist, hips, derriere—changed with regularity.

At the beginning of the twentieth century, the idealized female form in the West was sculpted by artifice, with restrictive corsetry and voluminous petticoats. During the century, with the exception of the 1950s, fashion's approach to the torso grew progressively more lenient. Developments in elasticized textiles that mold to the body's natural curves assisted contemporary designers, including Azzedine Alaïa and Hervé Léger, in realizing their paradigms of the female form.

Although costume history is rife with sculptural manipulations of the figure, the symmetry of the human armature was rarely questioned. Rei Kawakubo, Yohji Yamamoto, and Issey Miyake, addressing the body as only part of the integral whole of the garment, have used asymmetry as the core design concept in creating garments that virtually stand alone—alternative forms dependent on, but not defined by, the body. Reminiscent of the architectonic turn-of-the-twentieth-century underwear, contemporary garments also rely on additive structures or structural textiles to create extensions to the natural silhouette and change the perceived shape of the body. The result may be an ingenious twist on the historical figure, a freestanding geometrical model, or a piece of kinetic sculpture.

Issey Miyake
"Futon" Jacket, fall/winter 1995–1996
Polyester/cotton plain weave with
polyester fill
Costume Council Fund
AC1996.158.3

*Constantly exploring the concept of
producing clothes from "one piece
of cloth," Issey Miyake referenced the
traditional Japanese padded coverlet,
or futon, with this winter jacket.
Like the futon, the form of this jacket is
a rectangle edged with a wide border
in a contrasting color. Unlike the futon,
tubular sleeves have been added and
metal grommets secure tassels that
typically are stitched to the corners
of a traditional futon.*

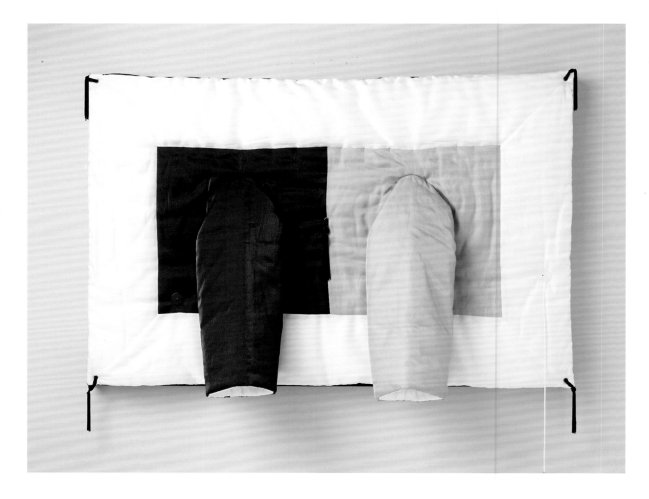

Issey Miyake
"Zig Zag" Dress, fall/winter 1994–1995
Polyester plain weave; pleated
and heat- and pressure-set
Costume Council Fund
AC1996.158.1

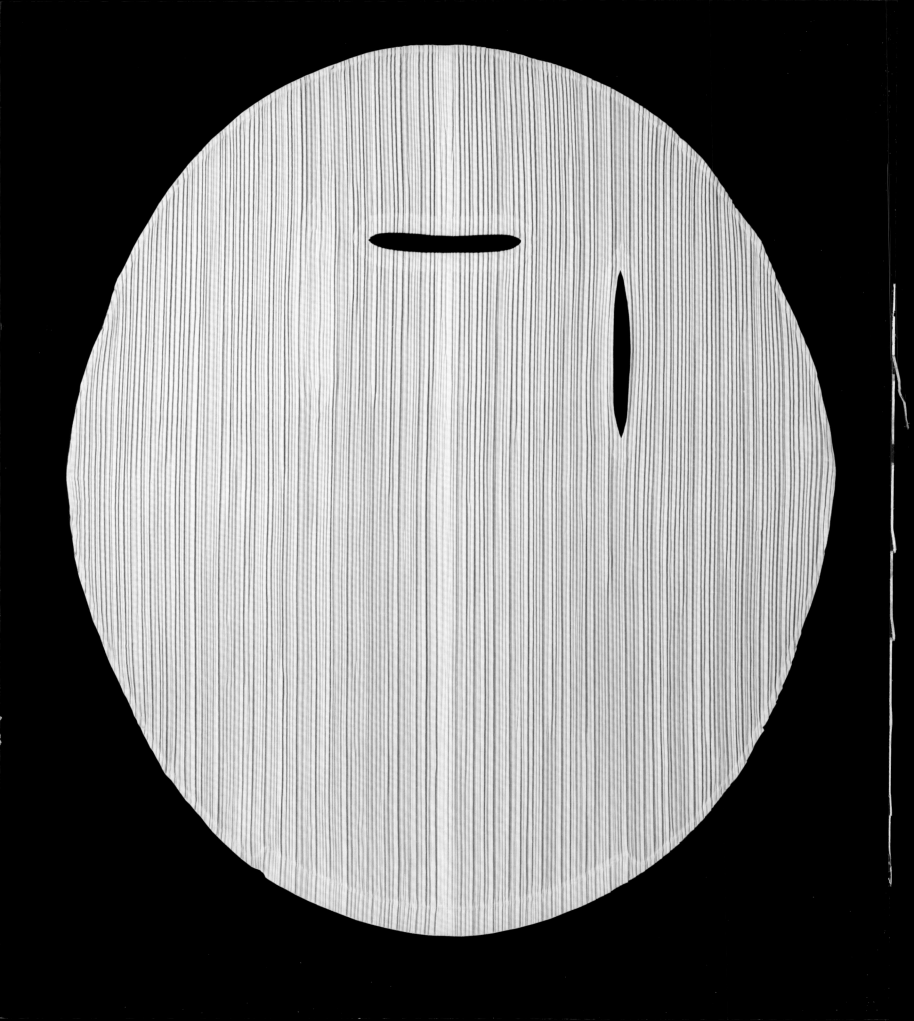

Issey Miyake

Two Dresses from the "Rhythm Pleats"
series, spring/summer 1990
Polyester plain weave; pleated and heat-
and pressure-set
Gift of the Miyake Design Studio
M.2007.101.4 and M.2007.101.5

*Inspired by the primary geometrical
shapes—circle, square, and triangle—
Issey Miyake fashions pliable structures
that seem like architecture to clothe the
flexible framework of the human body.
By imposing a two-dimensional
structure onto a three-dimensional
body, Miyake challenges traditional
fashion precepts of fit and proportion.
His garments, existing as simple
sculptural shapes off the body,
transform or are transformed by the
body when worn.*

Issey Miyake
Dress, c. 1986
Cotton/linen plain weave; printed
Gift of Mary Levkoff
AC1997.152.6

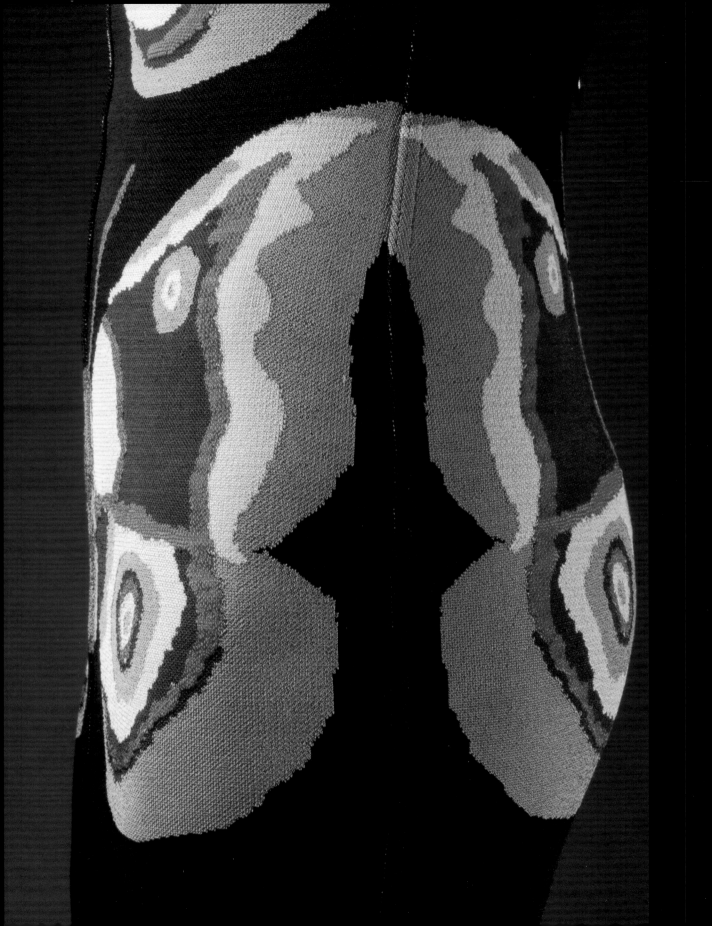

Azzedine Alaïa
Evening Dress, spring/summer 1992
Rayon and polyamide spandex knit
Gift of Sue Tsao
M.2006.71

*The study of sculpture was Azzedine
Alaïa's passionate pursuit, and seems an
obvious inspiration for his body-
conscious clothing. On his form-fitting
"cocoon," the brilliant colors of the
butterflies isolate and emphasize the
salient features of the female torso.*

Hervé Léger
Evening Dress, 1989
Rayon and lycra spandex knit
Purchased with funds provided by Nelly
Llanos Kilroy, Genevieve Chesebro,
and Cynthia Mitchel
AC1998.46.1

Azzedine Alaïa
Two-piece Evening Dress,
spring/summer 1992
Acetate knit
Purchased with funds provided
by Mr. and Mrs. John B. Kilroy
M.2007.22a–b

Based on the idealized 1950s hourglass-figure silhouette, but made without the constraining materials of corsetry, evening dresses by Hervé Léger and Azzedine Alaïa are constructed with knit horizontal strips wrapped around the body. The adroit manipulation of elasticized textiles has the quality, resilience, and objective of foundation pieces that romanticize the female shape.

Martin Margiela
For Maison Martin Margiela
Dress, spring/summer 2006
Silk plain-weave crepe
Purchased with funds provided
by Lanie Bernhard
M.2006.42

In 2005, Martin Margiela designed a number of garments made from varying lengths of the bandage fabric traditionally used for casts. This dress, a further development of that theme, resembles a blood-red "bandage" loosely wrapping the body while suggestively revealing its sensual form. The perfect alignment of the cylinder is pierced by sporadic gaps or "tears," left intentionally unstitched to suggest an unrolling bandage. The gaps expose the body beneath and intimate its vulnerability.

Issey Miyake
Jacket and Skirt from the "Superheroes"
series, 1996
Jacket: nylon knit with polyurethane
bonding; Skirt: nylon knit
Gift of Mrs. Nancy Stanton Knox
M.2000.139.1a–b

*Consistent with the tight-fitting
elasticized garments typically used
to clothe and emphasize the idealized
bodies of superheroes, this skirt hugs the
body, and the jacket is made of thick
yet lightweight synthetic fabric. Bulging
star-shaped insignias and muscular
shapes reference the colorful flash and
athletic sex appeal associated with
superheroes.*

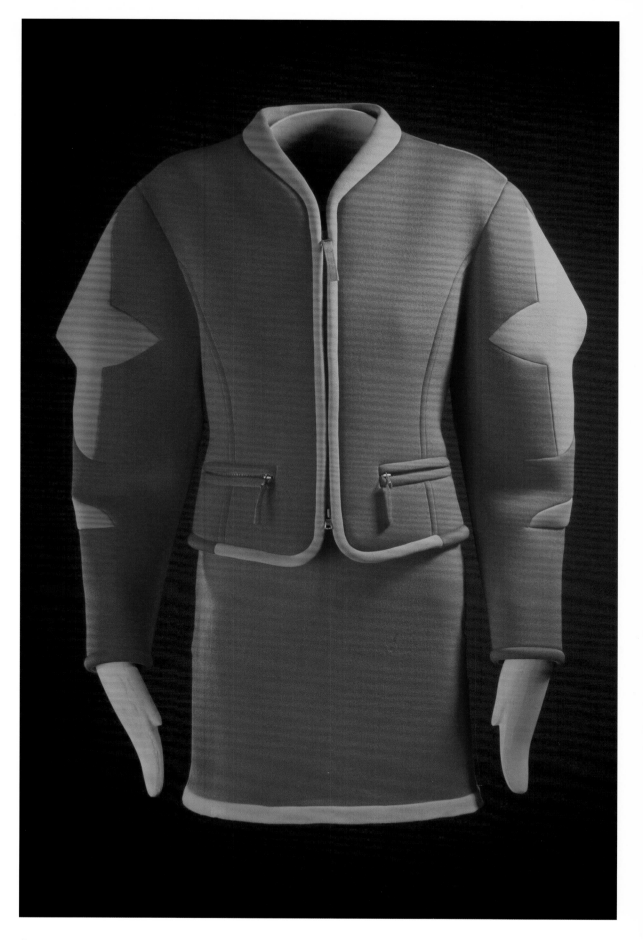

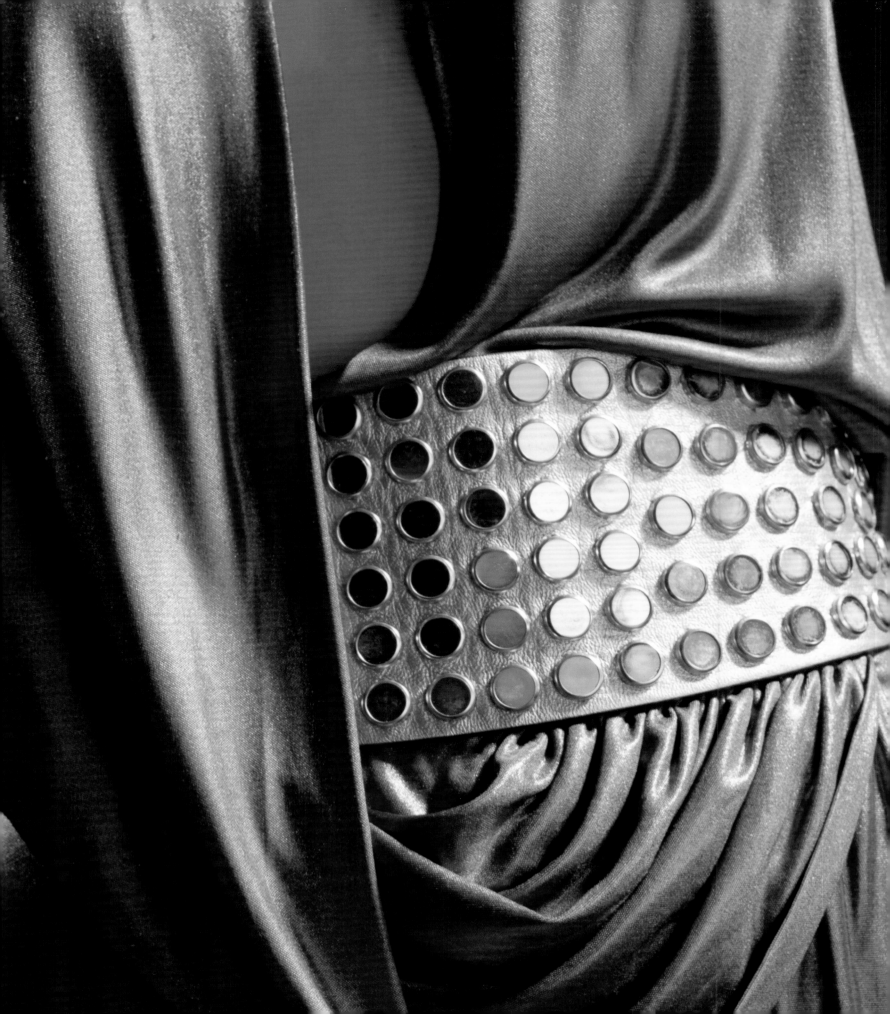

Frida Giannini
For Gucci
Evening Dress, fall/winter 2006–2007
Dress: lacquered viscose jersey;
Belt: leather and mirrors
Gift of Gucci
TR.15007a–b

Geoffrey Beene
Dress, 1992
Wool and acrylic double knit
Gift of Toby M. Horn in memory
of Rose K. Horn and Celia Rabin
M.2002.149.1

James Galanos

Two-piece Evening Dress, fall/winter
1989–1990
Overdress: rayon and nylon machine-
made lace, glass, and plastic beads;
Bodysuit: silk chiffon
Gift of James Galanos
AC 1997.248.17.1–.2

*Many contemporary designers explored
ideas of enclosure and exposure,
using the body as a source of form.
By choosing to enclose the figure in a
transparent glittering cylinder, leaving
opaque only the torso clothed in a
bodysuit, James Galanos successfully
demonstrated the visual dynamism
of negative and positive space. Frida
Giannini achieved the same dynamism
by exploiting the contrast between the
gleaming shimmer of fabric and the
subdued matte surface of skin. Geoffrey
Beene's dress, a study in positive and
negative space when clothing the body,
is a powerful structural shape when
standing alone.*

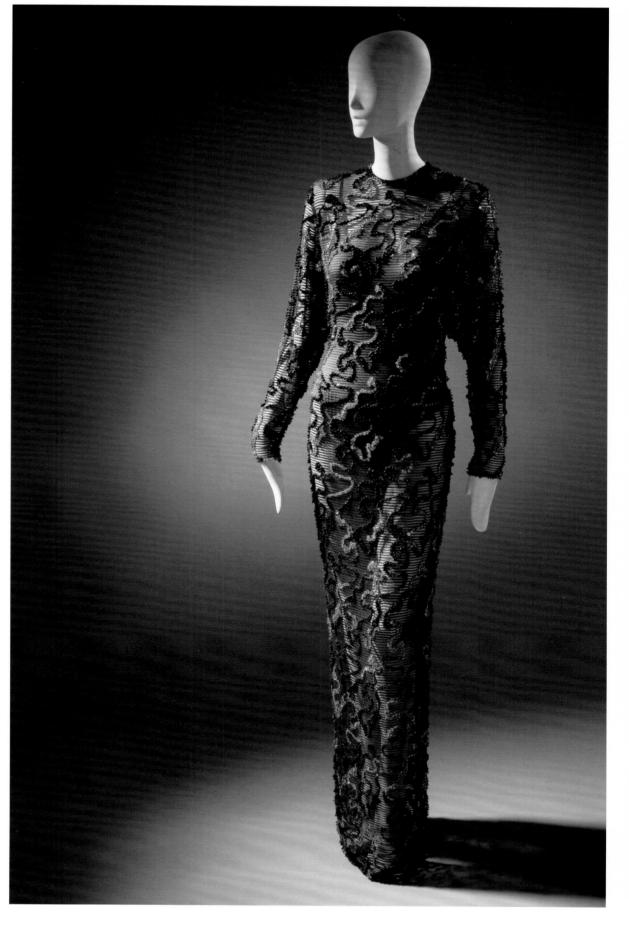

Martin Margiela
For Maison Martin Margiela
Blouse, fall/winter 2005–2006
Rayon and spandex knit
Costume and Textiles Special Purpose
Fund
M.2005.131

Martin Margiela envisioned the body in motion, contorted and waving wildly, as his pattern for this blouse. As a result, the blouse drapes in unpredictably abstract patterns when dressed on the body at rest.

Romeo Gigli

Jacket, c. 1988
Polyester and silk plain weave;
pleated and heat- and pressure-set
Gift of Helen Natalie Lewis
AC1997.199.5

*Romeo Gigli's interest in the
Renaissance may have influenced the
form of this jacket: the compacted
fabric on the arm creates a shape
similar to the short, puffed sleeve with
a narrow undersleeve characteristic
of 1560s women's dress, and the neck
and cuffs imitate ruffs from that period.*

Issey Miyake

"Mantis" Dress, fall/winter 1989–1990
Polyester plain weave; pleated
and heat- and pressure-set
Gift of Mrs. Cindy Canzoneri
M.2005.210.2

*Issey Miyake is often inspired by nature
and its creatures. Here, an enlarged
dress was hand-manipulated into
seemingly random angular folds prior
to being placed into a heated pleating
press. The transformed dress that
emerged when worn on a woman's body
took on a strange corrugated look
resembling the stiff but fragile shell and
wings of an insect, echoed in the collar
that appears to be in motion.*

Yohji Yamamoto
Dress, spring/summer 1990
Wool gabardine
Costume Council Fund
AC1999.8.5

*Shifting and fluid, the form of this dress
does not exist without a body, yet its
form does not correspond to the wearer's
body—thus creating an intriguing
tension between the two.*

Pierre Cardin
Evening Dress, late 1970s
Silk organza; printed
Gift of Mrs. Erich Koenig
M.2005.142.8

*Pierre Cardin frequently used the body
as a vehicle for sculptural form; his
fashion is derived from basic geometric
shapes—circles, triangles, and cubes.
The strength of these primary structures
can either showcase or obscure the body
beneath.*

Karl Lagerfeld
Dress, Hat, and Gloves, c. 1987
Dress: polished cotton twill and cotton
warp-faced plain weave; Hat: straw,
cotton warp-faced plain weave, and
grosgrain ribbon; Gloves: leather
and cotton warp-faced plain weave
Purchased with funds provided by
Ms. Marcy M. Engelbrecht, Mrs. Elliott
Horwitch, and Mrs. Walter Weisman
M.2006.23a–e

*Karl Lagerfeld creates a fashionable
optical illusion with geometric shapes
and contrasting stripes. The large
circular hat, heart-shaped bodice,
and descending cone of the skirt seem
to flatten the volume of the human
form, making a bold graphic statement
resembling a two-dimensional work
on paper.*

Gianfranco Ferré

"Cloud" Jacket Ensemble,
fall/winter 1986–1987
Jacket: silk organza plain weave;
Blouse: silk charmeuse;
Pants: silk and wool crepe
Gift of Gianfranco Ferré
TR.15009a-c

*This "Cloud" jacket, a veritable
structure of silk organza, paired with
very narrow pants, is a stunning
example of Ferré's sense of proportion
and capacity for balancing opposites—
traits honed in his earlier studies
in architecture and perfected in his
fashion design.*

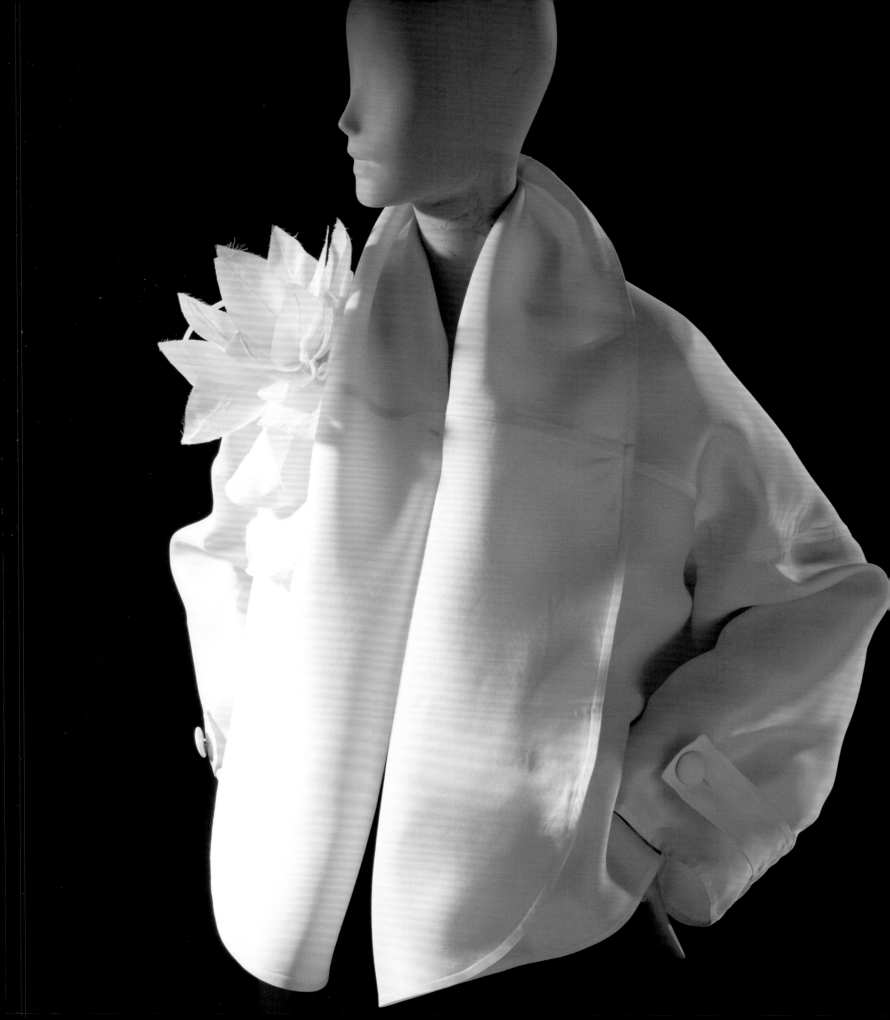

Issey Miyake

Two-piece Dress from the "Flower Pleats" series, spring/summer 1990
Polyester plain weave; pleated and heat- and pressure-set
Gift of Mr. and Mrs. H. Grant Theis
AC1998.161.1.1–.2

Strategically placed folded and pleated roundels are secured to this two-piece dress with large grommets. When placed on the body, the garment takes on sculptural shapes independent of the wearer's form.

Bustle
United States, c. 1885
Cotton machine-made lace, cotton twill,
and coiled wire
Anonymous gift
TR.7758.211

Bustle
United States, c. 1885
Cotton twill and wire
Anonymous gift
TR7758.209

The concept of beauty in form and silhouette of clothing is constantly changing. In the late nineteenth century, the bustle and bustle cage were used, in combination with corsetry and boning, to create an artificial version of the wearer's body form. The bust, hips, and buttocks were emphasized while the waist was diminished—this recipe for the "ideal" figure required the use of support structures.

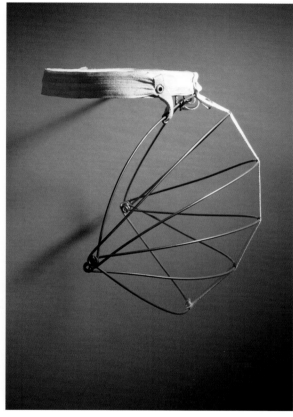

Wedding Dress
United States, 1876
Silk taffeta
Gift of John Ely Lathrop
and Marie Lathrop
38.19.1a–b

Rei Kawakubo
For Comme des Garçons
Two-piece Evening Ensemble,
fall/winter 1990–1991
Jacket: nylon and silver metallic
net with plastic trim; Skirt: nylon net
Costume and Textiles Special Purpose
Fund
AC1999.8.10.1–.2

*At the end of the nineteenth century,
stiff corsets and yards of fabric
were needed to realize the idealized
"S-curve" silhouette. Imitating the
S-curve at the end of the twentieth
century, Rei Kawakubo used stiff
synthetic materials to create volume
at the bodice front and simply wrapped
and tied a long length of net fabric for
a bustle effect.*

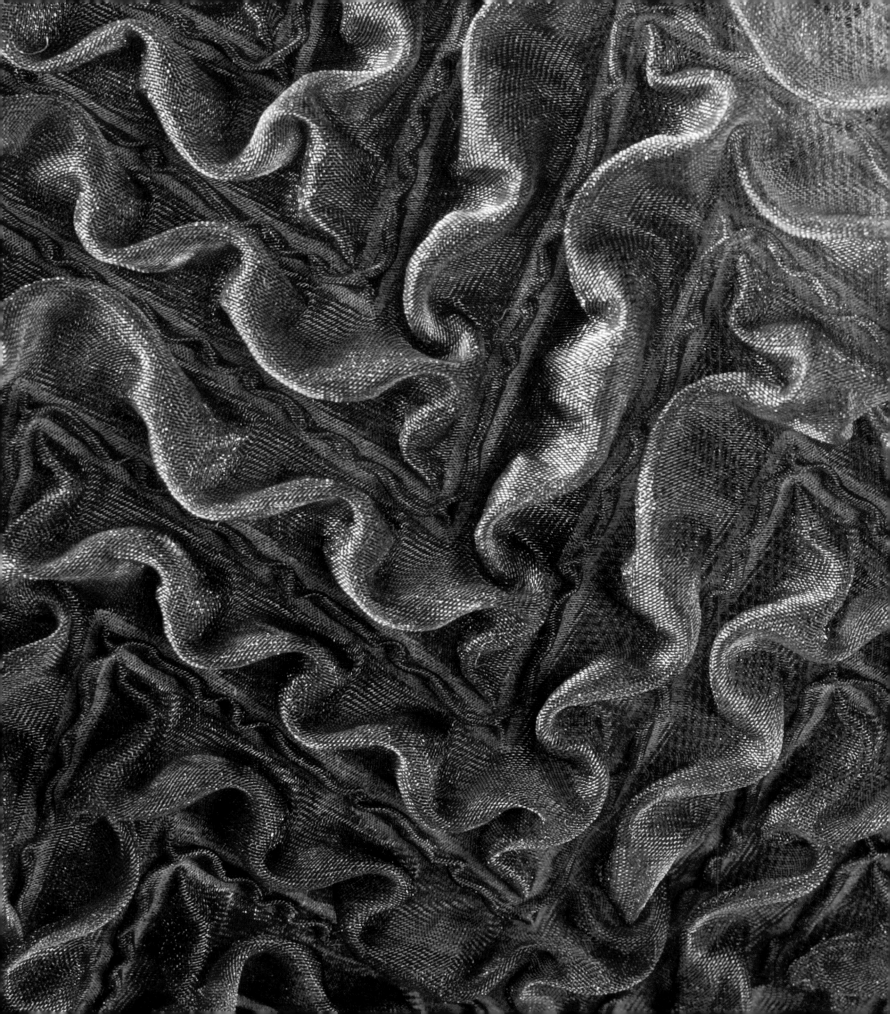

Rei Kawakubo

For Comme des Garçons
Two-piece Dress from "Body Meets
Dress, Dress Meets Body" collection,
spring/summer 1997
Overdress: crimped polyester plain
weave; Underdress: nylon net; Inserts:
polyurethane plain weave with feather
and down fill
Costume Council Fund
AC1998.87.3.1–.2

Blouse from "Body Meets Dress, Dress
Meets Body" collection, spring/summer
1997
Nylon net and acrylic knit; Inserts:
nylon knit with polyester fill
Gift of Caroline Schwarcz
AC1997.155.1.1a–c

*Challenging traditional notions of the
fashionable silhouette, Rei Kawakubo
placed shaped pads or "bumps" on
unexpected areas of the body in these
pieces from her controversial 1997
collection. She proposed a new aesthetic
by fusing the dress and the body into
a single soft, abstract sculpture.*

Downs & Bassett
"Empress Trail" Cage Crinoline,
1867–1869
Cotton patterned twill tape,
cotton-plain-weave-covered steel hoops,
and chamois
Anonymous gift
TR.7758.523

Yohji Yamamoto
"Hoop" Dress, fall/winter 1990–1991
Wool gabardine
Costume Council Fund
AC1996.158.5

Jacket, spring/summer 1999
Cotton twill
Gift of Lee and Mariana Ambrose
M.2005.140.7

Blouse, spring/summer 1999
Nylon knit
Gift of Carla Wachtveitl
M.2006.75

Yohji Yamamoto referenced the understructures that supported nineteenth-century cage crinolines in his "Hoop" dress. The monochrome black, patternless, trimless fabric places his version of a historical silhouette in a modern context. In a similar vein, his jacket utilized some of the same visual vocabulary to express a silhouette that exists outside the body of the wearer.

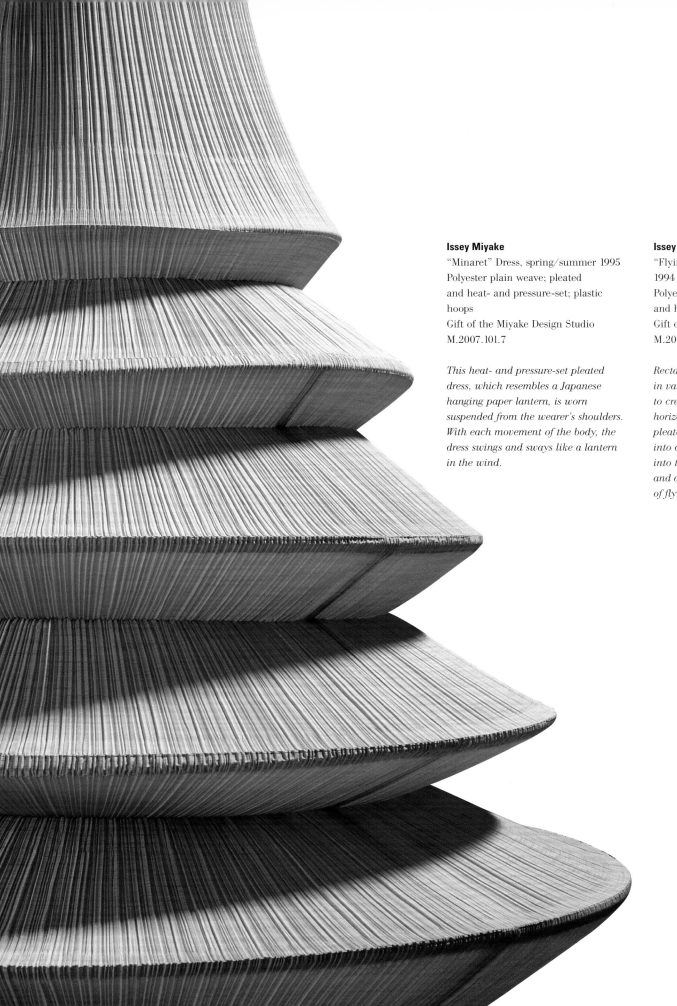

Issey Miyake

"Minaret" Dress, spring/summer 1995
Polyester plain weave; pleated
and heat- and pressure-set; plastic
hoops
Gift of the Miyake Design Studio
M.2007.101.7

*This heat- and pressure-set pleated
dress, which resembles a Japanese
hanging paper lantern, is worn
suspended from the wearer's shoulders.
With each movement of the body, the
dress swings and sways like a lantern
in the wind.*

Issey Miyake

"Flying Saucer" Dress, spring/summer
1994
Polyester plain weave; pleated
and heat- and pressure-set
Gift of the Miyake Design Studio
M.2007.101.3

*Rectangular pieces of polyester fabric
in various colors were stitched together
to create three lengths of patched
horizontal-striped yardage, then
pleated, gathered, folded, and placed
into a heated press. Stitched together
into tubular columns for body
and arms, the dress resembles a series
of flying saucers.*

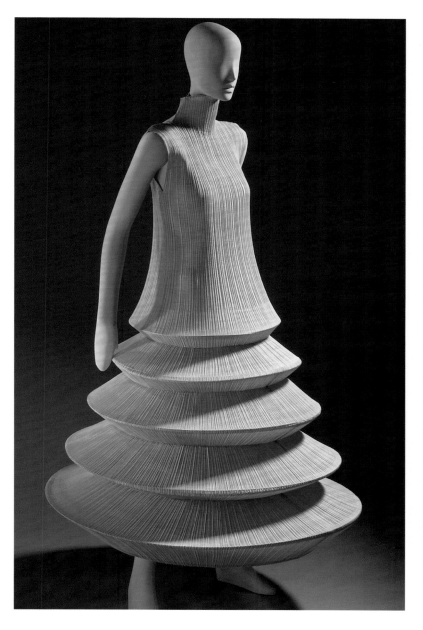

Sack-back Closed Robe
France, 1760–1780
Silk plain weave with supplementary
warp patterning; silk woven-braid trim
Purchased with funds provided
by John Jewett Garland
M.56.1.1

Gilbert Adrian
Evening Gown, 1951
Silk chiné taffeta and silk organza
patterned plain weave
Gift of Mrs. Leonard Firestone
CR.170.60-2

Christian Lacroix
Evening Dress from the "Luxe"
collection, spring/summer 1988
Silk chiné taffeta with silk grosgrain
ribbon trim
Costume Council Fund
AC1997.53.3

Thierry Mugler
Dress, 1994
Cotton twill
Costume Council Fund
AC1997.53.1.1–.2

During the eighteenth century, the
silhouette of French dress skirts evolved
into a wide horizontal profile.
The understructure that achieved this
shape was the panier *(basket).*
Manifested at the beginning of the
century as modest protrusions at the
hip, the panier *expanded to a width*
of six feet as the century progressed.
During the twentieth century, numerous
designers were inspired by the panier.
Gilbert Adrian used pleats and
petticoats to create the effect, while
Christian Lacroix chose textiles with
body and substance. Thierry Mugler
ingeniously allowed the stiffness
of heavy cotton twill and tailoring
to act as a structural device.

Designers wrestling with new concepts, evoking definitive positive or negative responses, are not committing transgressions against the established canons of fashion. These designers examine and deconstruct fashion's entrenched conventions, scrutinizing the origins of preconceptions—the "hows" and "whys" of traditional fashion rules—and consider any building block in the process fair game for subversion and conversion.

For some designers, historical sources are analyzed, taken apart, and re-created, yielding recombinant forms of old and new in unique configurations seen, for example, in trench coats by Burberry, Maison Martin Margiela, and Junya Watanabe. For others, social conventions are the subjects of inquiry. Society's ambivalence and fascination with underwear, for example, has been exploited by designers such as Vivienne Westwood and Dolce & Gabbana. Some designers make critical or confrontational assertions with their work or, like Franco Moschino, introduce wit and incongruity into their fashion statements. Issey Miyake chose to engage a series of artists because he sought fertile collaboration with other creative people whose concern was the body. A number of contemporary artists incorporate the complex visual language of fashion into their work because of its plethora of cultural, political, and economic associations.

Fashion is conceptual and functional; its compelling nature is that it can be either or both.

Underwear as Outerwear

The corset has been an element of dress since
medieval times. Constructed of such materials
as pierced metal, boiled leather, wood, linen, silk,
and elastic, these cages for both male and female
torsos have been reinforced variously with wire,
steel rods, whalebone, and, finally, lightweight
plastics.

The corset has always been considered underwear,
but at different times in the history of fashion its
design has been repeated in the form and
structure of the outer bodice, belying its exclusive
role as an intimate garment. Dress of the
eighteenth century followed the corset's line,
and the hourglass bodices of the late nineteenth
century mimicked the structure of the tightly
laced corset beneath. Contemporary designers,
such as Thierry Mugler, Vivienne Westwood, and
Dolce & Gabbana, have employed the corset as a
symbol of flamboyant female sexuality, a garment
of liberation to be chosen—not mandated—for
wear.

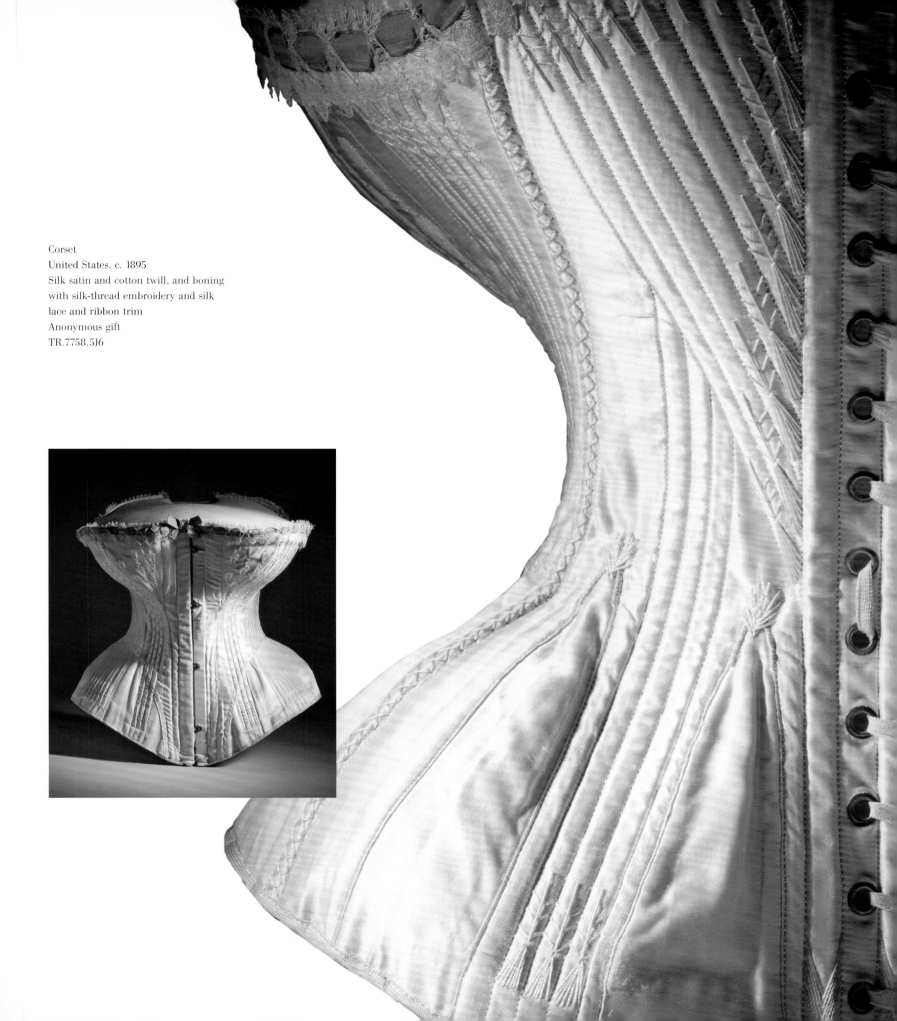

Corset
United States, c. 1895
Silk satin and cotton twill, and boning
with silk-thread embroidery and silk
lace and ribbon trim
Anonymous gift
TR.7758.516

Vivienne Westwood

"Stature of Liberty" Blouse,
fall/winter 1987–1988
Cotton and polyamide spandex
and machine-embroidered appliqué
Gift of Mr. and Mrs. Lee Ambrose
M.2002.185.18

"Mini-Crini" Skirt,
fall/winter 1987–1988
Cotton velveteen
Gift of Carole Raphaelle Davis
M.2003.153.4

In her fall/winter 1982–1983 "Nostalgia of Mud" collection, Vivienne Westwood showed bras worn on the outside of dresses. With this unequivocal role reversal, the designer created a new genre of underwear as outerwear. Her "Mini-Crini" first appeared in the spring/summer 1985 collection and further explored the genre, with eighteenth-century corsets and nineteenth-century hoop crinoline petticoats as inspiration for outerwear. Westwood's versions, however, are reinforced with woven plastic strips instead of the whalebone of the historical originals. The blouse's fabric stretches, thus mocking the corset's rigidity, and the hoop skirt is minuscule instead of massive like its predecessor.

Rei Kawakubo
For Comme des Garçons
Blouse and Skirt, fall/winter 2001–2002
Blouse: polyurethane and nylon and
cotton velveteen; Skirt: cotton
and rayon brocaded double weave and
cotton velveteen
Gift of Eva Elkins
M.2002.92a–b

Domenico Dolce and Stefano Gabbana
For Dolce & Gabbana
"Corset" Dress, fall/winter 1995–1996
Elastic, polyester, velveteen, and boning
Gift of Dolce & Gabbana
TR.15004.2

Thierry Mugler
Jacket, 1988–1990
Wool plain weave
Gift of Mrs. Cindy Canzoneri
M.2005.210.3

In Rei Kawakubo's updated and ironic pastiche of nineteenth-century underwear, function comes into question. An imitation corset is fashioned from imitation leather—soft to the touch and not meant to constrict. The hourglass contour and meticulous tailoring of Thierry Mugler's jacket recalls the shape and elaborate construction of fashion's time-honored undergarment, and scorning propriety, Domenico Dolce and Stefano Gabbana glorified the corset by turning it into a provocative dress.

Martin Margiela
For Maison Martin Margiela
Blouse (Remodeled Slip),
spring/summer 2003
Polyamide nylon knit slip
Gift of Jan Brilliot
M.2005.141.4

Since the 1950s nylon knit trimmed with lace has been associated with a woman's slip or lingerie and typically reserved as underwear—one's slip was never shown. Drawing a slip up from the waist and turning its skirt into a large cape collar, Martin Margiela transformed underwear, along with its associations, into respectable outerwear.

Rei Kawakubo

For Comme des Garçons
Three-piece Suit, fall/winter 2001–2002
Jacket: cotton and rayon brocaded
double cloth, cotton velveteen,
and nylon net with rayon and polyester
embroidery; Pants: wool brocaded
twill and nylon net with rayon and
polyester embroidery; Bra: wool twill,
nylon net, and elastic
Costume Council Fund
M.2002.65.1a–b

*The classic woman's tailored suit,
adapted from menswear, has been
interpreted and reinterpreted by
designers. Expanding on the
incongruous notion of underwear worn
on the outside, Rei Kawakubo placed
a decorative bra over this suit jacket.
She also made sections of the
"outside" completely transparent.
The embroidered net acts in concert
with opaque fabrics to form a collage
that both reveals and conceals the body
beneath.*

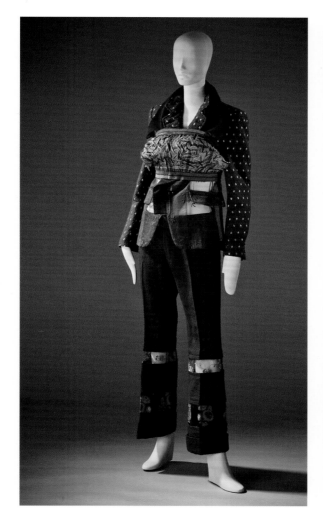
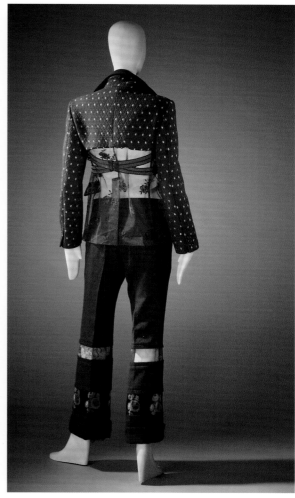

Junya Watanabe

For Comme des Garçons
Jacket, Shirt, and Pants,
spring/summer 2006
Jacket: cotton and acrylic patterned
twill; Shirt: cotton plain weave
with twill stripes; Pants: wool twill
Gift of Grace Tsao
M.2006.69.1, .2, .4

*This jacket is modeled after a man's
cutaway coat of the nineteenth century,
but its sleeves are inverted. The cuffs,
complete with buttons, are placed at the
garment's shoulder. And with the wider
armhole placed at the wrist, they
resemble the pagoda-shaped sleeves
fashionable in the 1850s. Pairing these
with trousers that suggest men's
eighteenth-century breeches, Junya
Watanabe designed a pastiche
of fashionable antecedents.*

Martin Margiela
For Maison Martin Margiela
Blouse, spring/summer 2005
Cotton plain weave
Gift of Ricki Ring
M.2005.143

Jeans, spring/summer 2003
Cotton denim and metallic paint
Gift of Ellen Olivier de Vezin
M.2006.113

*The elements of a tailored shirt or
blouse have become almost as standard
as a uniform: the placement of collar,
sleeves, buttons, and pocket remains
constant, even if fabric, color, or
patterns change. For this examination
of the blouse's form, Martin Margiela
rotated the standard parts a quarter
turn from their traditional placement
on the body, which created an unusual
drape on all sides and unsettled the
viewer's sense of balance.*

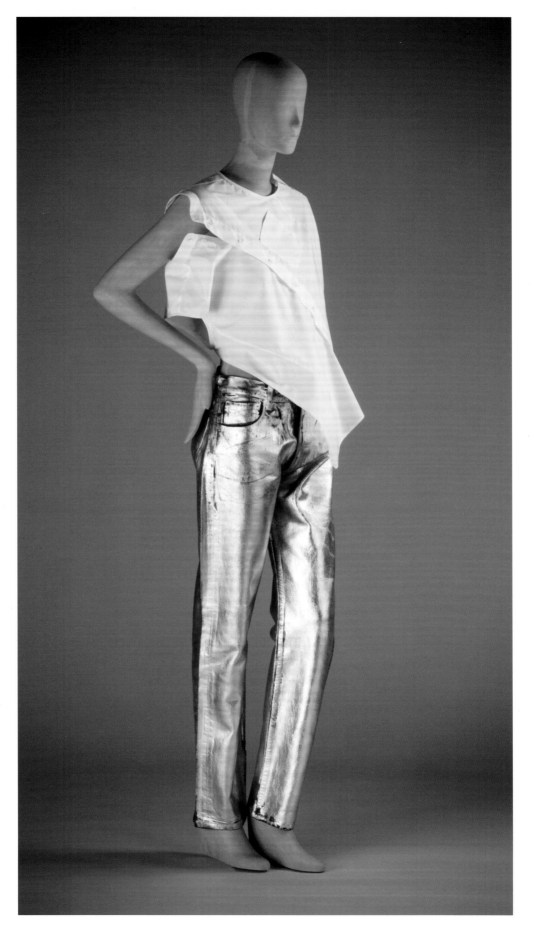

Martin Margiela

For Maison Martin Margiela
Blouse and Pants, spring/summer 2006
Blouse: silk crepe; Pants: polyester twill
Gift of Maison Martin Margiela
M.2006.74a–b

Metamorphosis is the subject of this
ensemble: a drastic change occurs
in form and symmetry from one side
of the garment to the other. Throughout
costume history, the symmetrical
treatment of limbs has been challenged
with innovative designs for separate
sleeves, but the marked disparity
between the two pant legs is startling.
Margiela created a pant/skirt hybrid—
an unsettling but elegantly integrated
transgression in dress.

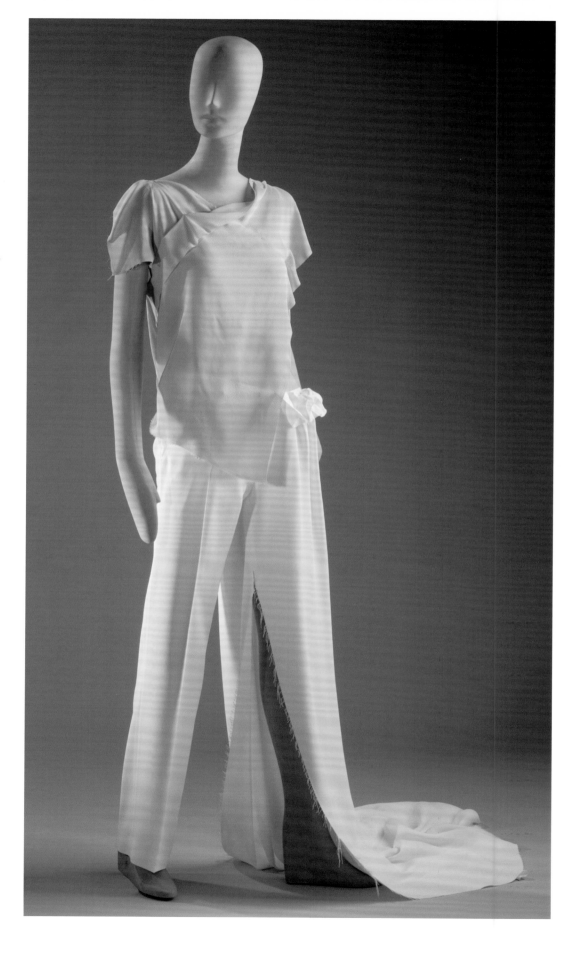

Martin Margiela

For Maison Martin Margiela
Trench Coat, spring/summer 2006
Cotton ribbed twill
Purchased with funds provided
by Hélène Bayer and Greta Popoff
M.2006.35

Pants, spring/summer 2005
Silk satin and cotton plain weave
Purchased with funds provided
by Jacqueline Avant
M.2006.24

*Martin Margiela's version of a trench
coat seems to be in transition: it
migrates, or dissolves, from one style
into another. One side, like a standard
trench coat, is completely tailored; the
other, inspired by the shape of a coat
casually thrown over the shoulder, is a
free-form untailored drape that can
be twisted or tied. Many of Margiela's
works are fascinating for the ambiguity
of their form and function.*

Junya Watanabe

For Comme des Garçons
Modified Trench Coat Jacket and Skirt
with "Avaricious" Shirt, spring/summer
2006
Jacket: cotton twill; Shirt: printed
cotton plain weave; Skirt: wool twill
Gift of Maureen Shapiro and Bennett
Rosenthal
M.2006.72.1a–b, .2, .3

*Displaced elements of the traditional
trench coat are used to create both the
construction and the decorative detail
of this outfit. The skirt's undulating
hem is composed of numerous trench
coat collars. The jacket is cut off and
wraps the shoulders and upper body,
instead of the waist, with its belt.
This association with bondage and the
shirt's photo-printed face with bloody
fangs pay homage to 1970s punk.*

Christopher Bailey
For Burberry Prorsum
Trench Coat, fall/winter 2003–2004
Cotton plain weave with polyurethane
coating
Gift of Susana Mercedes
M.2006.76

*The trench coat was developed in 1914
by famed outerwear maker Thomas
Burberry as an all-purpose coat that
could withstand the extreme weather
conditions seen in World War I's trench
warfare. The trench coat since has
become a fashion classic.*
*This cropped version retains all the
details characteristic of the original, but
the protective function has been
nullified. Burberry designer Christopher
Bailey also was referencing the
"Spencer," a very short-waisted jacket
without tails worn in the 1790s.*

Giorgio Armani

Suit and Blouse, spring/summer 1987
Jacket and Pants: linen and cotton twill;
Blouse: silk crepe
Gift of Giorgio Armani
TR.14987.1a–c

Suit and Hat, fall/winter 1990–1991
Jacket: silk crepe with metallic thread;
Pants: crepe-backed satin;
Hat: metallic cording
Gift of Giorgio Armani
TR.14987.2a–c

*Giorgio Armani is credited with
changing men's fashion by introducing
unstructured tailoring that achieved a
relaxed, yet perfectly streamlined fit.
His business and evening suits for
women were based on menswear and
admired for their androgyny and
modern elegance.*

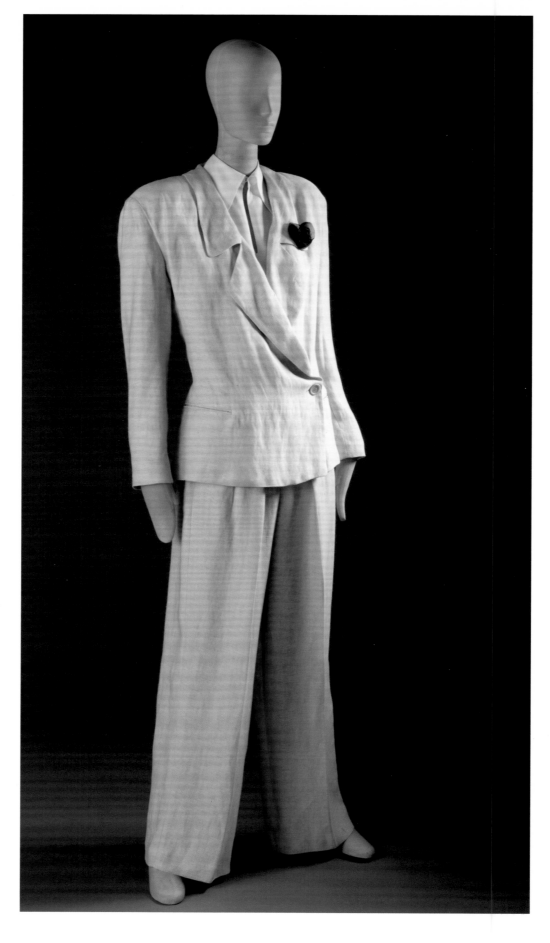

Yohji Yamamoto
Three-piece Ensemble,
spring/summer 1999
Modified Coat: polyester and silk
satin with rayon and nylon lace;
Blouse: rayon and nylon lace;
Pants: polyester and silk satin
Gift of Mr. and Mrs. Lee Ambrose
M.2002.185.39a–c

*Post-1980s attention to androgyny and
gender roles as expressed through dress
are illustrated in this ensemble, which
suggests the joining of the masculine
and the feminine through a marriage
of gendered garments—trousers
and lace, and suspenders with yards
of flowing feminine veil.*

Gianni Versace

Shirt, spring/summer 1992, and Skirt,
fall/winter 1991–1992
Shirt: cotton denim twill with brass
buttons; Skirt: silk twill and silk and
metallic lace; Belt: leather and metal
Gift of the Gianni Versace Archive
TR.15006a–c

*Gianni Versace's bold and extraordinary
juxtaposition of heavy denim and
leather with silk and lace—a rugged
male shirt with a luxurious* panier *skirt
referencing the dress of an eighteenth-
century woman—subverts conventional
ideas about materials suitable for
masculine or feminine dress.*

189

Domenico Dolce and Stefano Gabbana
For Dolce & Gabbana
Two-piece Suit and Blouse, fall/winter
1996–1997
Suit: worsted wool plain weave;
Blouse: cotton plain weave
Gift of Dolce & Gabbana
TR.15004.1a–c

The prescriptive roles of Sicilian women
are frequently interpreted in Dolce and
Gabbana's work: the traditional woman
in black, swathed in fringed shawls,
or the exotic sex goddess, corseted.
This pinstripe pantsuit for a woman
is evocative of the macho Sicilian
gangster.

Franco Moschino
Two-piece Suit, c. 1990
Linen and jute plain weave double cloth
Gift of Mrs. Cindy Canzoneri
M.2005.210.4a–b

*Franco Moschino vocalized his intention
to bring fashion, a system in which
he was actively involved, into crisis.
With this suit, he criticized the overly
branded icons of conventional fashion,
alluding to Chanel's signature boxy
silhouette but exaggerating the scale
of the buttons. By using fashion to make
a statement against itself, Moschino
questioned the values and practices
of the existing fashion system.*

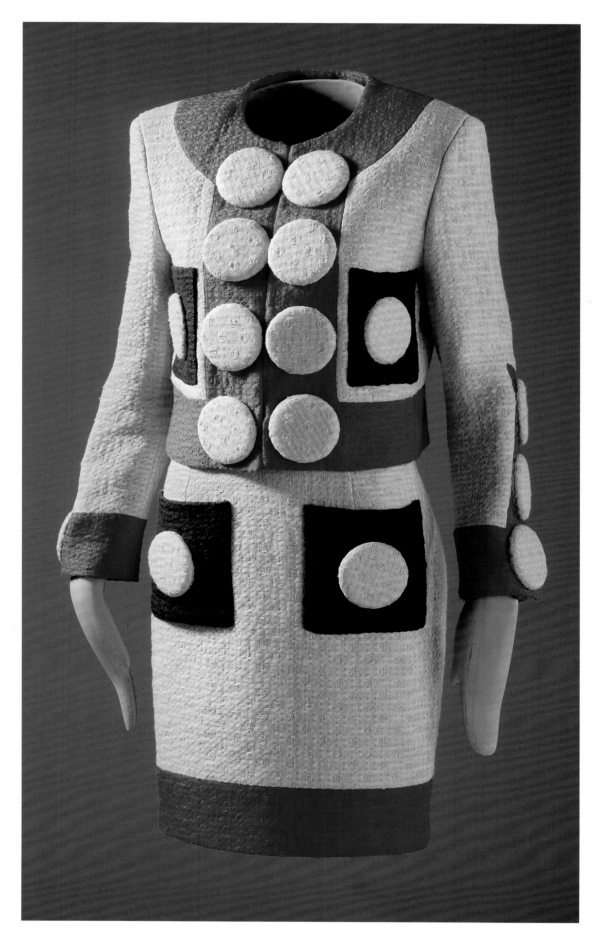

191

Jean-Charles de Castelbajac
"Pasta" Ensemble, fall/winter
1991–1992
Jacket: wool waffle weave; Skirt: wool;
Buttons and Necklace: silver metal
Costume Council Fund
M.2006.25a–c

Franco Moschino

"Dinner Jacket" Ensemble, fall/winter
1989–1990
Wool, wool and acetate, linen,
and metal flatware
Gift of Leslie Prince Salzman
M.2005.82.1a–c

*With these ensembles, Jean-Charles
de Castelbajac and Franco Moschino,
respectively, appropriated forms and
signifiers from the culinary world and
used them to clothe the body they
would typically nourish.*

Jean-Charles de Castelbajac
"Postcard" Skirt, mid-1980s
Silk gazar; hand-painted
Purchased with funds provided
by Cathy Bachrach
M.2006.30

Jean-Charles de Castelbajac's "postcard"
skirt can be transformed through the
simple act of buttoning or unbuttoning,
allowing the wearer to reveal all or part
of the imagery or text.

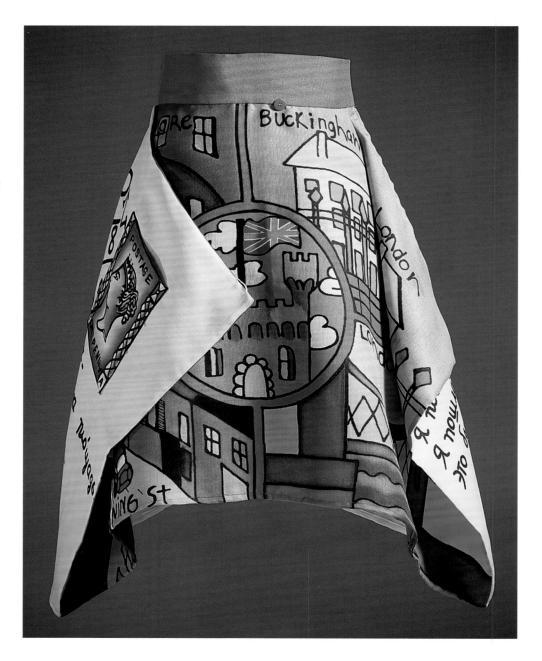

Miuccia Prada
For Prada
Dress, fall/winter 2005–2006
Silk, roller-printed
Costume Council Fund
M.2007.21.1

Miuccia Prada's work is characterized by the unusual combination of opposites, reflected in the dynamic interplay of black and white on this dress. The unique, free-form pattern is achieved with roller printing.

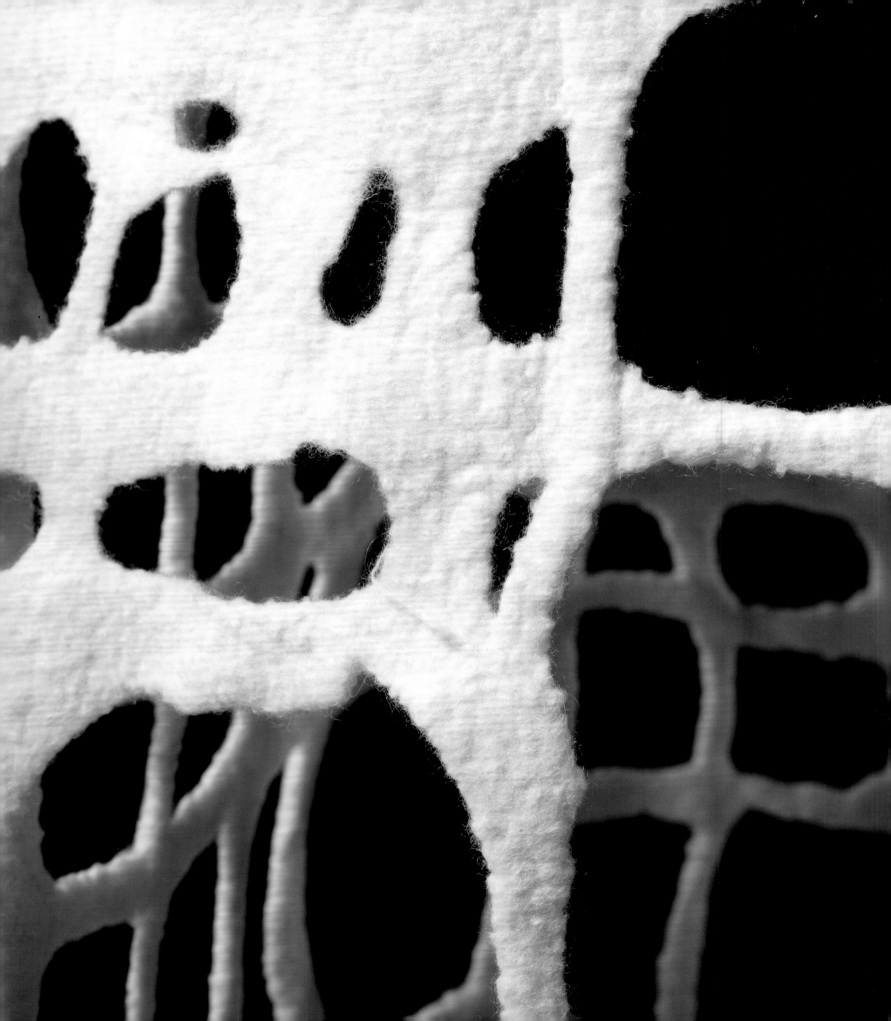

Andrea Zittel

"White Felted Dress #3" from A–Z Fiber
Form Uniforms, 2002
Wool; hand-felted
Purchased with funds provided
by David and Susan Gersh
M.2004.204

"White Felted Dress #6" from A–Z Fiber
Form Uniforms, 2002
Wool; hand-felted
Costume Council Fund
M.2004.185

*Addressing issues of self-sufficiency,
sculptor and installation artist Andrea
Zittel in 1991 started her ongoing
"A–Z Personal Uniform" project, which
consists of a succession of "perfect"
dresses meant to be worn for six months
at a time. In her "A–Z Fiber Form
Uniform" series, Zittel chose material
in its rawest form—unspun wool
fibers—that she hand-felted into
dresses, eliminating the need to cut
and sew fabric.*

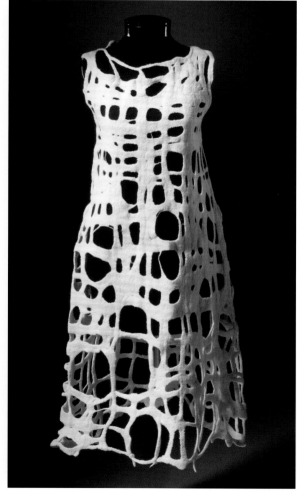

"Pleats Please
Issey Miyake Guest Artist Series"

In 1994, Issey Miyake launched his "Pleats Please" label, composed of basic clothing pieces designed to be practical yet stylish enough to complement his signature-label garments. Before pleating, these polyester garments are several times larger than the final product. They are sandwiched between two pieces of paper and hand-fed into a heat press. What emerges is permanently pleated clothing that stretches to adapt to the shape of the wearer, but also has enough textural substance to take its own independent forms. Between 1996 and 1999, Miyake invited four contemporary artists to use "Pleats Please" garments as blank canvases. The artists chose body imagery from their own work and collaborated with Miyake's design staff to transfer those images onto the garments. The resultant creations focused on the human figure—images of a body worn on another body. Each work is interesting, playful, and beyond what either Miyake or the individual artists would have created on their own.

Issey Miyake and Yasumasa Morimura
Blouse and Dress from "Pleats Please
Issey Miyake Guest Artist Series No. 1,"
1996
Polyester knit; printed and pleated
and heat- and pressure-set
Gift of Jun I. Kanai
AC1999.104.1–.2

*Contemporary Japanese artist Yasumasa
Morimura (born 1951) appropriates
images from famous historical artists
and reproduces them in his own designs.
In the late 1980s, he created self-portrait
works inspired by* La Source, *an 1856
painting by the French neoclassical
painter Jean-Auguste-Dominique Ingres
(1780–1867). For his computer-processed
photographic* Portrait (La Source III),
*Morimura inverted and superimposed
half of his body onto the lower half*

*of the Ingres image of the woman
in* La Source. *The resultant arresting
image presents contrasts between
female and male, original and copy,
painting and photography, and past
and present. When printed on a dress
and worn, the image moves in accord
with the wearer.*

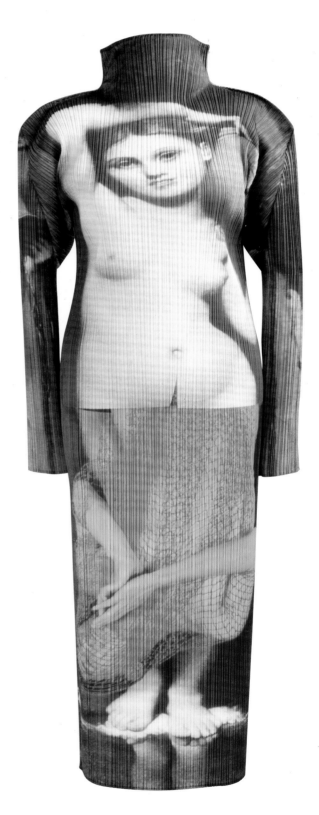

Issey Miyake and Nobuyoshi Araki
Issey Miyake and Nobuyoshi Araki
Two Dresses from "Pleats Please Issey
Miyake Guest Artist Series No. 2," 1997
Polyester knit; printed and pleated
and heat- and pressure-set
Gift of the Miyake Design Studio
M.2007.101.1 and M.2007.101.6

Nobuyoshi Araki (born 1940) is one
of Japan's most controversial
contemporary art photographers.
His images are autobiographical, based
on the theme of memory, and often
incorporate images of women. Araki's
oeuvre is well represented in these
"Pleats Please" dresses. The artist's
self-portrait was printed on a dress after
the garment was pleated; when
stretched onto the wearer's body, his
image fractures. The brooding woman's
image, which wraps around one side
of the dress, was printed prior to the
garment being pleated and appears
when worn by the wearer. Both images
move in and out of focus as the wearer
moves.

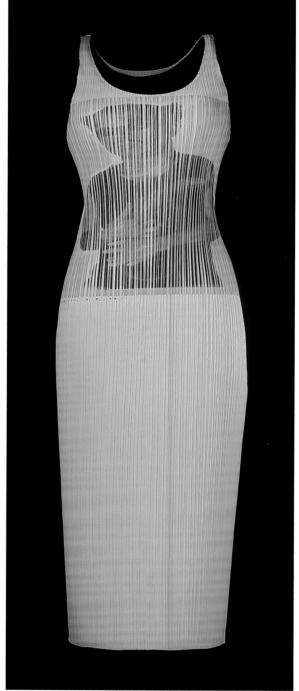

Issey Miyake and Tim Hawkinson

Dress from "Pleats Please Issey Miyake
Guest Artist Series No. 3," 1998
Polyester knit; printed and pleated
and heat- and pressure-set
Gift of Jun I. Kanai
AC1999.104.3

*Los Angeles–based artist Tim
Hawkinson (born 1960) examined
disparate methods of representing the
body on his collaborative "Pleats
Please" garments.
Hangmanofmycircumference—a 1995
self-portrait that illustrates the profile of
the artist's body divided into three-
centimeter thick "sections" on graph
paper—was printed onto an oversized
dress before it was placed in a heated
pleating press. The original image takes
on different dimensions after the
garment is pleated and again when it is
worn, creating a unique body that
is neither the artist's nor the wearer's.*

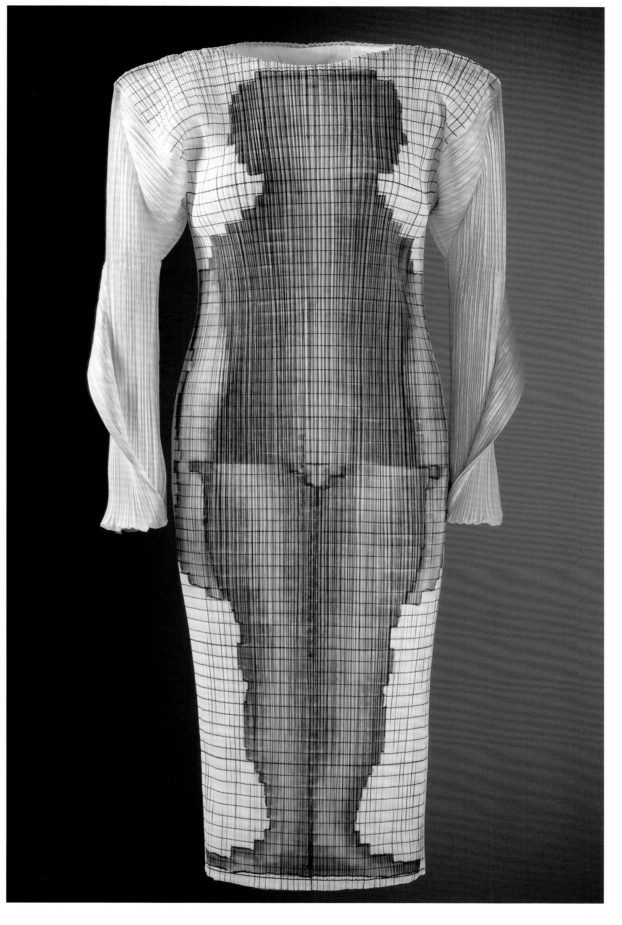

Issey Miyake and Tim Hawkinson
Jumpsuit from "Pleats Please Issey
Miyake Guest Artist Series No. 3," 1998
Polyester knit; printed and pleated and
heat- and pressure-set
Gift of Dale and Jonathan Gluckman
AC1999.99.1

Tim Hawkinson's 1992 sculpture Eye
Globe *was constructed of articulating
baby doll eyes embedded into a globe.
When switched on, the globe slowly
rotated and onlookers could see and
hear the dolls' eyelids slowly open and
shut. Images of magnified eyes from*
Eye Globe, *printed onto a jumpsuit after
it was pleated, expand and contract
with the movements of the wearer.*

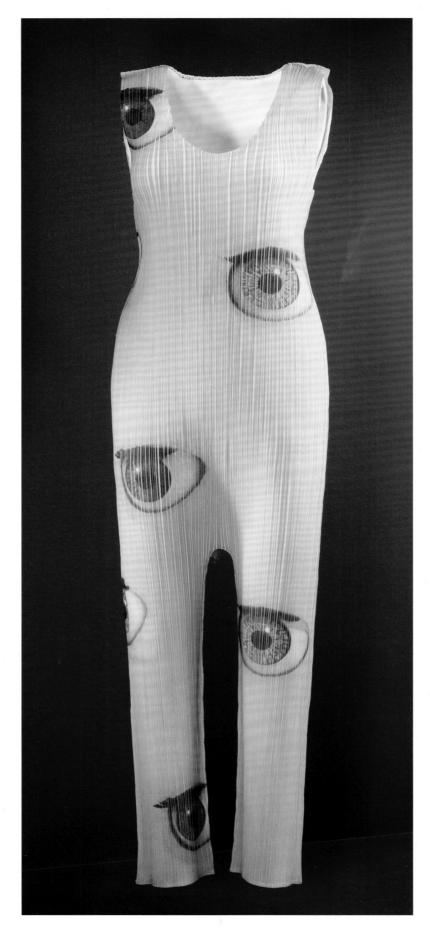

Issey Miyake and Cai Guo-Qiang
Jumpsuit from "Pleats Please Issey
Miyake Guest Artist Series No. 4," 1999
Polyester knit; printed and pleated
and heat- and pressure-set
Gift of Alice A. Wolf
AC1999.124.1

*Chinese artist Cai Guo-Qiang (born 1957)
investigates the properties of gunpowder
in his work. At the 1999 Paris opening
of the exhibition* Issey Miyake Making
Things, *Guo-Qiang performed* Dragon:
Explosion on Issey Miyake Pleats Please.
*Pleated garments in various forms were
spread out on the floor in the shape
of a dragon, the Chinese symbol of life.
A trail of gunpowder was sprinkled
over the clothing and ignited, and the
burned and singed garments were later
hung in the exhibition. Select burn
patterns were photographed and printed
onto new "Pleats Please" garments,
such as this jumpsuit.*

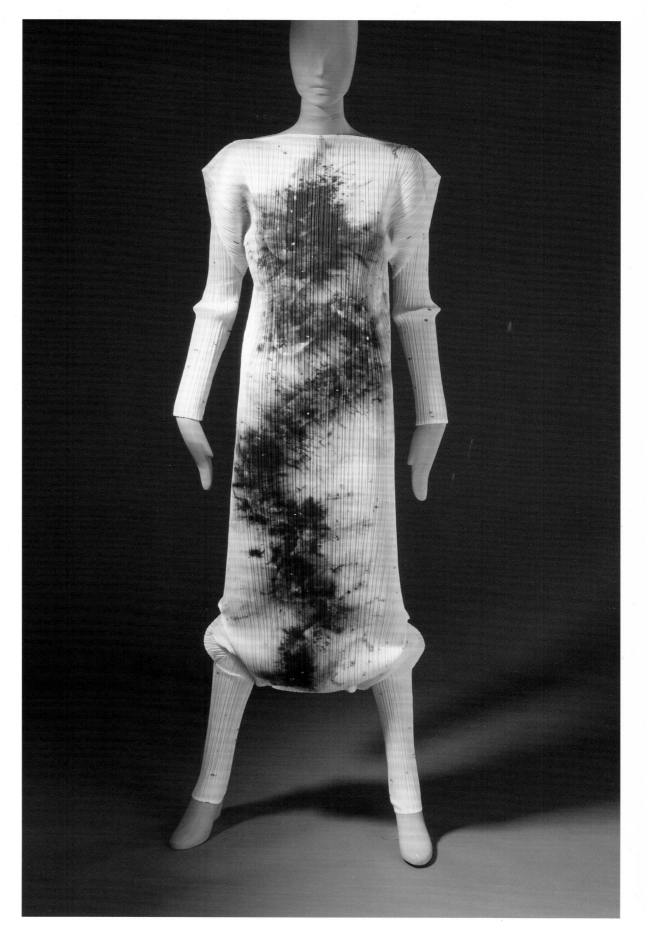

Biographies

Adrian, Gilbert
(United States, 1903–1959)
After studying at the New York School of Fine and Applied Art (later Parsons School of Design), New York and Paris, Adrian worked as a film and theater designer in New York from 1921 to 1928. He achieved worldwide recognition during his years as head costume designer for Metro-Goldwyn-Mayer studios in Hollywood (1928–1939). From 1941 to 1952 in Los Angeles, Adrian produced his custom and ready-to-wear line, Adrian Ltd.

Alaïa, Azzedine
(Tunisia, born c. 1940)
Before working with Guy Laroche from 1957 to 1959, Alaïa spent several years as a dressmaker's assistant in Tunis. He made couture clothing for many years before gaining prominence in the 1980s for his distinctive body-conscious clothing. Alaïa's first ready-to-wear collection appeared in 1980. From 2000 to 2007 he formed a partnership with Prada. This collaboration in designing shoes and leather goods is still ongoing, even though Azzedine Alaïa has regained financial control of his firm.

Armani, Giorgio
(Italy, born 1934)
Armani is one of the great innovators of contemporary fashion, offering an identity to women by creating his famous "power suit," the career woman's outfit. He renewed menswear by removing the elements of traditional tailoring such as shoulder pads and interfacing, and by creating a more relaxed, yet elegant style. Armani's first collection came out in 1975. From that moment on Armani has become synonymous, around the world, with elegance. His more economical line, Emporio Armani, was launched in 1981. He has been honored with several exhibitions of his work and numerous industry, fashion, and community awards.

Bailey, Christopher
(England, born 1971)
Bailey came to the venerable British firm of Burberry in 2001 as creative director after five years as senior womenswear designer at Gucci. After receiving an MA in fashion from London's Royal College of Art, he worked for Donna Karan from 1994 to 1996. Bailey has radically changed the conservative image of Burberry, while continuing to capitalize on many of its classic pieces, such as the trench coat, for inspiration.

Balenciaga, Cristóbal
(Spain, 1895–1972)
Considered one of the twentieth century's most important fashion designers, Balenciaga opened his business, named Eisa, in Barcelona (1922) and in Madrid (1932). Maison Balenciaga opened in Paris in 1937. After a successful career, embraced by an international clientele for the sculptural quality of his clothes and the virtuosic technique of his clothing construction, the designer closed his house in 1968. The company has since seen Michel Goma and Josephus Thimister as head designers, and is now experiencing a renaissance under the artistic direction of Nicolas Ghesquière.

Beene, Geoffrey
(United States, 1927–2004)
Starting his education in medicine in 1943, Beene turned to fashion in 1947 and studied at Traphagen School in New York. From his first collection in 1963, his clothing was characterized by its close relationship with the body, either fluid and clinging or remarkably sculptural. Although masterfully cut and tailored, his work was frequently unconventional in color, texture, and design.

Cardin, Pierre
(Italy, born 1922)
From 1945 to 1950 Cardin worked with the house of Paquin, then with designers Elsa Schiaparelli and Christian Dior, solidifying his mastery of the art of tailoring. Following his premier collection in 1951, the designer was the first couturier to produce a ready-to-wear collection in 1959. He became famous for his futuristic 1964 "Space Age" collection, and for his provocative revisions of the traditional men's business suit. Although he was known for using the body more as a vehicle for minimalist sculptural form, Cardin also designed feminine evening wear in diaphanous, colorful prints.

Castelbajac, Jean-Charles de
(Morocco, born 1949)
With his mother, Castelbajac founded the ready-to-wear firm Ko & Co. in 1968. His work has been based on explosive color, pop art, op art and comic book imagery, graffiti, and texts printed on simple architectural garments. Working with artists, he produced the first "painted dresses" in 1982. His designs have been realized in several media, from home furnishings to liturgical garments, and his work has been featured in many international exhibitions.

Chalayan, Hussein
(Cyprus, born 1970)
Chalayan is considered one of the most cerebral designers working today. His graduate collection in 1993 at Central Saint Martins College of Art and Design in London set the stage for a career of avant-garde collections based on recurrent themes of technology, transformation, oppression, and cultural displacement. From 1994 to 2001 Chalayan also designed for TSE, New York, and Asprey, London. The designer's work has been in a number of international exhibitions, and he has many awards to his credit, including British Designer of the Year in 1999 and 2000.

Dessès, Jean
(Egypt, 1904–1970)
The designer's first couture collection was shown in 1937 in Paris. An expert tailor with a sense of the garment as sculpture, Dessès experimented with many types of fabrics and created elegant suits and daywear, but he was best known for his intricately draped and pleated silk chiffon evening dresses.

Dior, Christian
(France, 1905–1957)
One of the most influential designers of the twentieth century, Dior began his career as a dealer of modern art. He worked as an illustrator and designer with Robert Piguet and Lucien Lelong and opened his own house in 1946. His first collection in 1947, called the "New Look," was considered revolutionary because of its contrast to the menswear look of the previous war years, and Dior achieved international prominence. His highly constructed clothes were distinguished by sculptural contours, luxurious fabrics, and exquisite tailoring. After his death, a succession of designers continued as the house's artistic directors: Yves Saint Laurent (1957–1959), Marc Bohan (1960–1989), Gianfranco Ferré (1989–1996), and John Galliano (1997 to present). Many major museums have since exhibited the revered designer's legacy.

Dolce, Domenico
(Italy, born 1958),
Stefano Gabbana
(Italy, born 1962)
The interests that direct the aesthetic of these two designers are centered in Sicily, the birthplace of Dolce. Themes that recur in their collections are based on the image of women in Sicily wearing traditional dress, as well as the stereotypes of the Latin sex goddess and the Sicilian gangster. Founded in 1985, the house expanded into

menswear in 1990, then into eyewear, fragrances, footwear, children's clothing, swimwear, and home furnishings.

Ferragamo, Salvatore
(Italy, 1898–1960)
An apprentice shoemaker from 1907 to 1912, Ferragamo moved to the United States in 1914, setting up a family business in Santa Barbara (1914–1923). Ferragamo's shoes, remarkably innovative in design, technique, and use of unusual materials, earned him a clientele that included a number of Hollywood stars; he remained in Hollywood until 1927, and then returned to Florence. Following his death, his family assumed the business and expanded worldwide. His inventions included the platform and the "invisible" shoe. The Salvatore Ferragamo Museum in Florence is a repository for his production.

Ferré, Gianfranco
(Italy, 1944–2007)
After graduating in architecture, Ferré worked as a jewelry and accessory designer from 1969 to 1973, and he unveiled his first collection in 1978. From 1989 to 1996, Ferré was the head designer for the house of Dior. The designer's work was informed by an architect's sense of proportion, symmetry, and balance, as well as the interaction between these dynamic forces. Ferré was the recipient of numerous artistic and civic awards, and his work has been featured in many exhibitions.

Fortuny, Mariano
(Spain, 1871–1949)
Born Mariano Fortuny y Madrazo in Grenada, Fortuny was the son of a well-known painter. Most famous for his innovations in the production of textiles, Fortuny created his distinctive, intricately pleated "Delphos" dress in 1907 and patented the process in 1909. He developed a number of printing methods to make lavish velvets, stenciled in gold and silver and based on patterns of Italian textiles of the fifteenth and sixteenth centuries. He also excelled in painting and in many other fields of the fine arts, including printmaking, photography, and theater design, and during his long career, registered a number of industrial patents for inventions in these areas.

Fujiwara, Dai
(Japan, born 1967)
Receiving a degree in textile design in 1995, Fujiwara then took a position in textile design and research at Miyake Design Studio. Since 1997, he has worked with Issey Miyake on the various collections of A-POC (A Piece of Cloth)—a revolutionary rethinking, through the use of computer technology, of the process of making garments.

Galanos, James
(United States, born 1924)
Galanos studied at the Traphagen School in New York, worked in various roles for Hattie Carnegie, Jean Louis (as a sketch artist for film costume), Robert Piguet, and Davidow from 1944 to 1949, and finally launched his first collection in 1951. The designer's work has always been respected for its masterful tailoring, quality fabrics, and attention to detail; it is ready-to-wear made to the standards of haute couture. The subject of museum exhibitions, Galanos has also received many of the fashion industry's highest accolades.

Galliano, John
(Gibraltar, Spain, born 1960)
Galliano's 1984 graduate collection from Central Saint Martins College, named "Les Incroyables," accorded him status as an up-and-coming designer, and he launched his first collection in 1985. In 1995 he was appointed chief designer for Givenchy, and in 1997 he presented his first collection as creative director for womenswear at Dior. Hailed for his extravagant interpretations of historical period dress, Galliano also inventively manipulates the costume of various world cultures and incorporates the imagery of current events into his work, thus overturning conventional assumptions of what is "appropriate" in fashion design.

Gaultier, Jean Paul
(France, born 1952)
Gaultier trained with Pierre Cardin, Jacques Esterel, and Jean Patou, and founded his own line in 1978. Lionized in the press as the "bad boy" of fashion, Gaultier is known as an iconoclast. With each new collection, he satirizes or obliterates the stereotypes associated with haute couture, but he maintains a reputation for precision and innovation in construction. He is known for his unorthodox use of materials and for breaking down the barriers of gender. He is one of a very few designers, for example, who have created skirts for men. Gaultier created his first haute couture collection in 1997, and since 2004 he has also designed womenswear for Hermès.

Gernreich, Rudi
(Austria, 1922–1985)
After emigrating to the United States in 1938, Gernreich studied in Los Angeles until 1942, when he became a dancer and costume designer for the Lester Horton dance company. From 1951 to 1959 he worked with William Bass, Inc., and he established his own company in 1964. The visionary designer challenged the rigid rules of shape and construction of the 1950s with his unconstructed knitwear and brilliant color combinations, which were considered startling for the period. Most famous for his 1964 "topless" bathing suit, Gernreich set the standard for fashion in the social, political, and aesthetic context of the 1960s and 1970s.

Gigli, Romeo
(Italy, born 1949)
Gigli was schooled in architecture but pursued a career in fashion instead, producing a collection of handknits in 1972 and showing his first women's collection in 1981. His garments are created in luxurious fabrics—silk, metallics, and stenciled velvets reminiscent of Fortuny—that betoken the designer's romantic vision nurtured by his interest in historical painting and exotic imagery.

Grès, Madame
(France, 1903–1993)
Germain Alix Barton's early desire to be a sculptor is manifested in her silk jersey gowns inspired by classical Greek dress. From 1934 to 1940 she designed for the house Maison Alix, then opened her own business as Madame Grès in 1942. The designer's evening dresses, meticulously pleated and elaborately draped, were her signature garments from the 1930s until she retired in 1988.

Gucci, House of
(Italy, founded 1921 by Guccio Gucci, 1888–1953)
Frida Giannini
(Italy, born 1972)
The famous luxury brand in fine leather goods was established by Guccio Gucci, and the family-run business expanded successfully into clothing, accessories, and household furnishings until the 1980s, when it suffered financial problems. A revival of the company's prestige came in the 1990s with the arrival of American Tom Ford; after Ford's departure in 2002, a creative team, including Frida Giannini, took his place. Giannini became creative director of the house in 2005.

Hishinuma, Yoshiki
(Japan, born 1958)
Hishinuma attended the Bunka Fashion

College but withdrew to join the Miyake Design Studio in 1978. In 1984 he showed his collections in Tokyo, established his own company in 1987, and in 1992 launched the Yoshiki Hishinuma label in Japan and showed his first collection in Paris. Known in the 1980s for his huge, wind-blown garment constructions, Hishinuma has concentrated on developing highly innovative textiles. Using natural and chemical processes, he explores the broad possibilities of form and surface finishes with synthetic fibers.

Izukura, Akihiko
(Japan, born 1942)
Izukura graduated from Doshisha University in Kyoto with a degree in economics, but he has spent his professional life as a textile weaver. Practicing his philosophy of harmony with nature, he uses natural materials and processes exclusively, dyeing silk by hand in subtle colors. He has developed innovative techniques for weaving and braiding fiber, but also uses Karakumi, an ancient Japanese method of knotting. Izukura directs his company, Hinaya, from Kyoto and teaches workshops all over the world.

James, Charles
(England, 1906–1978)
Although born in England, James has always been considered the quintessential American designer. He began as the milliner "Charles Boucheron" in Chicago from 1924 to 1928, then became the dressmaker "E. Haweis James" in London and Paris from 1929 to 1939. The designer established his own label in 1942, then resided permanently in the United States thereafter. James was known and esteemed for his strikingly sculptural garments. An artist of the human form and an engineer of its dressing, he created monumental eveningwear, coats, and suits that were brilliantly proportioned and fastidiously tailored.

Kamali, Norma
(United States, born 1945)
After her education at Fashion Institute of Technology in New York, Kamali worked as a freelance designer and boutique owner until she established OMO (On My Own) in 1978. Kamali was influenced by street fashion and was acutely aware of the frenetic lifestyle of the modern woman, so she used materials like parachute nylon and knit fabrics for both casual and eveningwear, making the jumpsuit and bodysuit essential components of fashionable dress in the 1980s.

Kawakubo, Rei
(Japan, born 1942)
After graduating in fine arts in 1964, Kawakubo worked in advertising for a chemical and textiles company. She founded Comme des Garçons in 1973, developed Homme menswear in 1978, and showed her first women's collection in Paris in 1981. Since then, the designer has pursued a career distinguished by unrelenting challenges to conventional notions of the fashionable silhouette, elegance, and rules of garment construction. Her cerebral approach informs every aspect of her men's and women's clothing lines, as well as the design, architecture, and presentation in her boutiques all over the world. Kawakubo's work is in the collections of international museums and has been included in many international exhibitions.

Kelly, Patrick
(United States, 1954–1990)
Kelly studied history at Jackson State University, Jackson, Mississippi, and fashion design at Parsons School of Design in New York. After several jobs in the fashion industry, Kelly went to Paris in 1980, worked as a freelance designer, and launched his ready-to-wear-collection in 1985 and his couture collection in 1987. The designer's work is known for explosive color, bold graphic patterns, innovative application of decorative accessories, and especially for its humorous yet creative use of unusual elements for inspiration.

Krizia
(Italy, founded 1954)
Mariuccia Mandelli
(Italy, born 1933)
Mandelli cofounded Krizia with Flora Dolci in 1954, and they showed the first named collection in 1957. After attaining international recognition with her debut collection at the Palazzo Pitti in 1964, Mandelli expanded into knits, launching Krizia Maglia in 1967. She designed children's clothing and menswear. Her work is known for garments featuring unusual combinations of widely diverse fabrics and textures, inventive pleating, and application of colorful animal motifs.

Lachasse Ltd.
(England, founded 1928)
The respected British couture house was established by Digby Morton, who acted as head designer from 1928 to 1933, followed by Hardy Amies from 1934 to 1939, Michael Donellan from 1941 to 1952, and Peter Lewis-Crown, who was made artistic director in 1964. Lachasse Ltd.'s strength was the consummate skill in construction and the streamlined look of its tailored suits. The company is based in London and has added millinery to its repertoire.

Lacroix, Christian
(France, born 1951)
Lacroix pursued an education in art history and museum studies from 1973 to 1976, but turned to fashion—working at Hermès, Guy Paulin, and then from 1981 to 1987 as chief designer at Jean Patou. In 1987 he established his own couture house and showed his first collection. Lacroix's work is known for its baroque opulence, with its references to the extravagant fashion of the eighteenth century, lavish use of saturated color, and emphasis on luxurious fabrics—all made modern by idiosyncratic and irreverent touches.

Lagerfeld, Karl
(Germany, born 1938)
In 1955, at age seventeen, Lagerfeld started working at Pierre Balmain, and then moved to Jean Patou and served as artistic director there from 1958 to 1963. While at Chloé (1963–1973; 1993–1997), he also designed furs for Fendi, and he continues to create all the collections for that house. Beginning as head designer for Chanel in 1983, Lagerfeld revived the prestigious brand by appropriating the emblems of Coco Chanel's iconic style and reinventing them in a contemporary idiom. In 1984 the designer established Karl Lagerfeld, followed by Lagerfeld Gallery, and in 2004 he ventured into mass marketing by joining retailer H&M.

Léger, Hervé
(France, born 1957)
Beginning in 1975, Léger worked with a number of stellar houses and designers—Lagerfeld, Chanel, Diane Von Furstenberg, Lanvin, Chloé—before producing his first collection in 1992. His signature designs—"bender" dresses made of hand-sewn elastic strips—encapsulated and formed the female figure into an idealized shape, sexy and statuesque. In 1999 Léger left the company, and in 2001 he opened his boutique, Hervé L. Leroux, in Paris.

Margiela, Martin
(Belgium, born 1957)
One of the "Antwerp Six," Margiela studied at the Royal Academy of Art in Antwerp, and after moving to Paris in 1984, worked with Jean Paul Gaultier until 1987. In 1988, Maison Martin Margiela was founded. The designer interrogates

every aspect of fashion; schooled in couture techniques, he employs these skills to realize "dissident" concepts of construction. Vintage garments are recycled and hand-worked into unique pieces, and many of his designs are inspired by the unlikely or unusual use of textiles or garment parts. From 1997 to 2003, Margiela also designed the women's collections for Hermès.

Marras, Antonio
(Italy, born 1961)
In 1988 Marras launched his first ready-to-wear collection, and in 1996, the first haute couture collection under his own name. He was appointed head designer for Kenzo in 2003. The works from the designer's Laboratorio are unique, made by hand from various textiles and treatments. Using deconstructive methods, such as ripping and staining, on the same garment with meticulously executed hand embroidery, Marras creates ensembles that marry opposites: architectural shapes and patterns composed of exquisitely delicate materials and techniques.

McQueen, Alexander
(England, born 1969)
The designer learned the art of tailoring on Savile Row and sharpened his expertise by working successively with theater costumers Angels and Bermans in London, and with designers Koji Tatsumo in Tokyo and Romeo Gigli in Milan. His "Jack the Ripper" graduation collection for Central Saint Martins College attracted wide attention from the press; McQueen launched his first collection in 1996, and in the same year was appointed head designer for Givenchy, where he remained until 2001. The frequently provocative and erotic nature of his clothing has been displayed in sensational runway shows laden with confrontational thematic content, and it has kept McQueen in the avant-garde of contemporary design.

Missoni, Rosita
(Italy, born 1931)
Ottavio Missoni
(Croatia, born 1921)
Starting with a small factory in 1954, and the establishment of the Missoni label in 1958, this knitwear firm attained worldwide recognition in the 1960s and 1970s for garments of exceptional quality and technological innovation, distinctive for their bold geometric patterns in brilliant colors. Daughter Angela Missoni introduced her first collection in 1993; she became the firm's creative director in 1997. Missoni has been the recipient of numerous fashion awards and has been the subject of international exhibitions.

Miyake, Issey
(Japan, born 1938)
After studying art in Tokyo, Miyake went to Paris in 1965 to study couture. From 1966 to 1970 he worked for Laroche, Givenchy, and Geoffrey Beene; he then showed the first Miyake collection in Paris in 1973. Hailed as one of the most creative and independent designers of the twentieth century, Miyake has always explored the relationship of the body to its covering, producing garments of remarkable fantasy and indecipherable complexity. His "Pleats Please" line was inaugurated in 1993, and "A-POC" (A Piece of Cloth), which focuses on computerized production of knit clothing, was introduced in 1999. Both lines display his ability to design clothes with the versatility to suit modern lifestyles.

Moschino, Franco
(Italy, 1950–1994)
After studying fine arts, Moschino worked as a designer and illustrator until 1982, when he opened his company Moonshadow, and he introduced Moschino Couture! in 1983. Always a conspicuous critic of the fashion system, he mixed and twisted classic styles with visual puns, slogans, and incongruous imagery in his surreal approach to clothing design. Moschino launched his diffusion line, Cheap & Chic, in 1988. After his death in 1994, Rossella Jardini assumed the role of creative director of the house.

Mugler, Thierry
(France, born 1948)
At fourteen, Mugler danced with the Opéra de Rhin. After moving to Paris, he worked as a freelance designer and professional photographer, established his own label in 1974, and made his first couture collection in 1992. His work has been influenced by comic-book superheroes and the theatricality of 1950s Hollywood glamour. Mugler's suits and gowns mold the idealized proportions of an exaggerated hourglass figure; their stark sculptural quality makes them timeless—associated with pure form instead of seasonal caprice.

Prada, Miuccia
(Italy, born 1949)
The Prada name was established in 1913 by two brothers who made fine leather goods. Miuccia joined the firm in 1971 after studying political science and acting; she made an immediate commercial success with her design for a black nylon backpack. After taking over the company in 1978, she introduced ready-to-wear in 1989, the Miu Miu line in 1992, and menswear in 1994. With her husband, CEO Patrizio Bertelli, Prada amassed a succession of partnerships that culminated in an enormous fashion conglomerate. The designer's work is distinctive for its individualism, which rejects the tyranny of seasonal style. Prada exploits unusual combinations of textures, materials, and methods of construction that stamp her ready-to-wear lines with a hand-crafted appearance.

Pucci, Emilio
(Italy, 1914–1992)
After studying at universities in Italy and the United States, Pucci received a Ph.D. in 1941. In the 1940s, he developed lines of fashionable sportswear, and his chic ensembles of tunics and pants in saturated Mediterranean colors were part of the first Pucci shop, which opened in 1949 in Capri. He became famous for his "Capri pants" and simple dresses of swirling, delicately drawn textile designs so representative of the brilliant color and energetic patterns of the 1960s and 1970s. The designer received numerous artistic and civic awards. After his death, his daughter Laudomia became artistic director; there has since been a revival of international interest in the famous Pucci prints, now designed by Matthew Williamson. The sixtieth anniversary was celebrated this year.

Sudo, Reiko
(Japan, born 1953)
Sudo and Junichi Arai (Japan, born 1932) cofounded the textile studio, Nuno Corporation, in 1984. Sudo has explored traditional and experimental techniques, natural and chemical processes, and combined incompatible and unusual materials to create remarkably innovative textiles. The designer's work has been included in many international exhibitions, and she is represented by several major museums.

Toyoguchi, Takezo
(Japan, born 1942)
After graduating from the Bunka Fashion College in 1965, Toyoguchi worked for Haute Couture Hosono, and in 1982 founded Takezo, his women's collection for export. In 1986 he showed Takezo for Men, followed by three women's collections in 1987 (Takezo Toyoguchi Fashion Office), 1995 (Takezo), and 1999 (Takezo Toyoguchi). The designer also teaches fashion design at Nagoya University of Arts and Sciences.

Treacy, Philip
(Ireland, born 1967)

Renowned for his unique millinery, Treacy started his education in 1985 at the National College of Art and Design in Dublin, then graduated from London's Royal College of Art in 1990. In 1991 he opened a showroom in London and started making couture hats for Chanel, and in 1994 he opened his own boutique. Treacy has also done couture hats for Alexander McQueen and Givenchy. His wildly imaginative sculptural headwear has been the subject of a number of museum exhibitions, and Treacy has been a repeat recipient of the award for British Accessory Designer of the Year.

Versace, Gianni
(Italy, 1946–1997)

After studying architecture in the mid-1960s, Versace worked as a freelance designer from 1968 to 1977. He showed his first womenswear collection in 1978, and menswear the following year. His aggressively sexy dresses revealed and enhanced the bodies of well-known actresses, and Versace contracted with supermodels and celebrities to promote his flamboyant style. Vivid colors, luxurious fabrics, and bold pattern mixes were hallmarks of Versace's work. Following his untimely death, his sister Donatella succeeded him as creative director of the company.

Watanabe, Junya
(Japan, born 1961)

Watanabe graduated from the Bunka Fashion College in Tokyo in 1984 and went directly to work at Comme des Garçons as a pattern maker and designer of knits and menswear. Although employed by Comme des Garçons, Watanabe also has his own label; his first womenswear collection was shown in Tokyo and Paris in 1992, and his first menswear in Paris in 2001. The designer is intensely interested in the effects of new materials, and the combination of complementary or incompatible opposites. The abstract silhouettes of his clothes result from textural layers and complex piecing of garment parts.

Westwood, Vivienne
(England, born 1941)

From the moment she opened her shop, Let It Rock, in 1971 with Malcolm McLaren, Westwood has had a long line of successes in her mission to shock the establishment. In the period from 1972 to 1980, she and McLaren owned a number of boutiques devoted to the antifashion inspired by the punk movement—bondage and fetish, vinyl and rubber, and shirts screened with provocative texts of sexual and political content. Her 1982 "Nostalgia of Mud" collection featured bras on the outside of dresses, and some of her work, such as corsets and "Mini-Crini" skirts, is based on underwear as outerwear. Always original, Westwood has brilliantly and shamelessly reinvented the silhouettes of costume history for the modern audience.

Yamamoto, Yohji
(Japan, born 1943)

Yamamoto began his education by studying law, but he graduated instead from the Bunka College of Fashion in 1969. He launched his own label in Japan in 1971 and showed his first Paris collection in 1981. With fellow Japanese designers Rei Kawakubo and Issey Miyake, Yamamoto was part of the startling assault on the Paris fashion establishment in the early 1980s. By introducing asymmetrical garments, loosely wrapped and layered rather than cut, tailored and fitted, Yamamoto fused the aesthetics of traditional Japanese clothing with aspects of Western fashion, creating a radically different concept of couture. In addition to his eponymous label, the designer produces Y's for Women and Y's for Men.

YEOHLEE
(United States, founded 1981)
Yeohlee Teng
(Malaysia, born 1951)

After studying fashion at New York's Parsons School of Design, Teng launched her label, YEOHLEE, in 1981. Her work has been characterized as "intimate architecture" because of its concise geometrical design and creative exploration of the relationship between the body and the clothing that houses it. Her garments for the "urban nomad" are intriguing, for both aesthetic appeal and adaptability. In 2001, YEOHLEE: Supermodern Style was presented at the Fashion Institute of Technology, and the designer's work has been part of many exhibitions at venues such as Massachusetts Institute of Technology's Hayden Gallery, the Victoria and Albert Museum, and the Museum of Contemporary Art in Los Angeles.

Zittel, Andrea
(United States, born 1965)

Sculptor Andrea Zittel concentrates on examining the structures of everyday life—the actions and materials and rituals most necessary for living—creating, under the name A–Z Enterprises, all the elements of her own wardrobe, lifestyle, and environment. For one of her projects, Zittel made an extensive series of garments (A–Z Six-Month Seasonal Uniforms) in various handmade fibers and construction techniques that reexamine the appearance, function, and nature of clothing and its psychological connection to the wearer. Zittel studied sculpture and painting at San Diego State University and received an MFA from Rhode Island School of Design. Her work has been extensively published and exhibited internationally.

Note
Nobuyoshi Araki (Japan, born 1940), Cai Guo-Qiang (China, born 1957, active Japan 1986–1995, currently active New York), Tim Hawkinson (United States, born 1960), and Yasumasa Morimura (Japan, born 1951) are contemporary artists.

Selected Bibliography

Assouline, Yaffa, Martine Assouline, Sabine Bond, et al., eds. *Alaïa: Livre de Collection*. Paris: Assouline, 1992.

Baudot, François. *Thierry Mugler*. New York: Universe, 1998.

Beene, Geoffrey, James Wolcott, Marylou Luther, and Pamela A. Parmal. *Beene by Beene*. Laura Jacobs, ed. New York: Vendome Press, 2005.

Benbow-Pfalzgraf, Taryn, ed. *Contemporary Fashion*. Farmington Hills, MI: St. James Press, 2002.

Blow, Isabella, Philip Treacy, and Hamish Bowles. *Philip Treacy: "When Philip met Isabella."* New York: Assouline, 2002.

Bolton, Andrew. *The Supermodern Wardrobe*. Exh. cat. New York: Abrams; London: V&A Publications, 2002.

Braddock, Sarah E., and Marie O'Mahony. *Techno Textiles: Revolutionary Fabrics for Fashion and Design*. New York: Thames and Hudson, 1998.

Breward, Christopher. *Fashion*. Oxford: Oxford University Press, 2003.

Coleman, Elizabeth Ann. *The Genius of Charles James*. New York: The Brooklyn Museum, 1982.

Derycke, Luc, and Sandra Van de Veire, eds. *Belgian Fashion Design*. Ghent and Amsterdam: Ludion, 1999.

Deschodt, Anne-Marie. *Mariano Fortuny: Un Magicien de Venise*. Paris: Éditions du Regard, 2000.

Evans, Caroline. *Fashion at the Edge: Spectacle, Modernity and Deathliness*. New Haven and London: Yale University Press, 2003.

Evans, Caroline, Suzy Menkes, Ted Polhemus, and Bradley Quinn. *Hussein Chalayan*. Exh. cat. Rotterdam: NAi Publishers in association with Groninger Museum, 2005.

The Fashion Book. London: Phaidon, 1998.

Felderer, Brigitte. *Rudi Gernreich: Fashion Will Go out of Fashion*. Cologne: DuMont, 2000.

Frankel, Susannah. *Visionaries: Interviews with Fashion Designers*. New York: Abrams; London: V&A Publications, 2001.

Frisa, Maria Luisa, ed. *Italian Eyes. Italian Fashion Photographs from 1951 to Today*. Exh. cat. Milan: Charta & Fondazione Pitti Discovery, 2005.

Frisa, Maria Luisa, and Stefano Tonchi. *Excess. Fashion and the Underground in the '80s*. Exh. cat. Milan: Charta & Fondazione Pitti Discovery, 2004.

Fukai, Akiko, ed. *Fashion: The Collection of the Kyoto Costume Institute, A History from the Eighteenth to the Twentieth Century*. Cologne: Taschen, 2002.

Gan, Stephen. *Visionaire's Fashion 2001: Designers of the New Avant-Garde*. Alix Browne, ed. New York: Universe, 1999.

Giacomoni, Silvia. *L'italia della moda. Fotografata da Alfa Castaldi*. Milan: Mazzotta, 1984.

Golbin, Pamela. *Fashion Designers*. New York: Watson-Guptill, 2001.

Golbin, Pamela, ed. *Balenciaga Paris*. New York: Thames and Hudson, 2006.

Izukura, Akihiko. *Textiles of Akihiko Izukura*. Kyoto: Hinaya, 2001.

Jones, Terry, and Avril Mair, eds. *Fashion Now: i-D Selects the World's 150 Most Important Designers*. Cologne: Taschen, 2003.

Jones, Terry, and Susie Rushton, eds. *Fashion Now*. Cologne: Taschen, 2006.

Jouve, Marie-Andrée. *Balenciaga*. Text by Jacqueline Demornex. New York: Rizzoli, 1989.

Koda, Harold. *Extreme Beauty: The Body Transformed*. Exh. cat. New York: The Metropolitan Museum of Art, 2001.

Koike, Kazuko, ed. *Issey Miyake: East Meets West*. Tokyo: Heibonsha, 1978.

Mancinelli, Antonio. *Antonio Marras*. Venice: Marsilio & Fondazione Pitti Discovery, 2006.

Martin, Richard, ed. *Contemporary Fashion*. Detroit: St. James Press, 1995.

Martin, Richard, and Harold Koda. *Christian Dior*. Exh. cat. New York: Abrams; New York: The Metropolitan Museum of Art, 1996.

Martin, Richard, and Harold Koda. *Infra-Apparel*. Exh. cat. New York: Abrams; New York: The Metropolitan Museum of Art, 1993.

McCarty, Cara, and Matilda McQuaid. *Structure and Surface: Contemporary Japanese Textiles*. Exh. cat. New York: Abrams; New York: The Museum of Modern Art, 1998.

McDowell, Colin. *Fashion Today*. London: Phaidon, 2000.

McDowell, Colin. *Galliano*. New York: Rizzoli, 1998.

McDowell, Colin. *Jean Paul Gaultier*. London: Cassell, 2001.

Meij, Ietse, and Marie-José Raven, eds. *Yoshiki Hishinuma in the Fashion Gallery of the Gemeentemuseum The Hague*. Exh. cat. Zwolle, The Netherlands: Waanders Publishers; Den Haag, The Netherlands: Gemeentemuseum Den Haag, 1999.

Milbank, Caroline Rennolds. *Couture: The Great Designers*. New York: Stewart, Tabori and Chang, 1985.

Mitchell, Louise, ed. *The Cutting Edge: Fashion from Japan*. Sydney: Powerhouse, 2005.

Miyake, Issey, Dai Fujiwara, and Mateo

Kries. *A-POC Making: Issey Miyake and Dai Fujiwara*. Berlin: Vitra Design Museum; Tokyo: Miyake Design Studio, 2001.

La moda italiana. Dall'antimoda allo stilismo. Milan: Electa, 1987.

La moda italiana. Le origini dell'alta moda e la maglieria. Milan: Electa, 1987.

Moffitt, Peggy. *The Rudi Gernreich Book*. New York: Rizzoli, 1991.

Mower, Sarah. *Twenty Years: Dolce and Gabbana*. Milan: 5 Continents Editions, 2005.

Mulvagh, Jane. *Vivienne Westwood: An Unfashionable Life*. London: HarperCollins, 1998.

Penn, Irving, ed. *Irving Penn Regards the Work of Issey Miyake: Photographs 1975–1998*. Boston: Bulfinch, 1999.

Rossellini, Isabella, introduction. *Ten Years of Dolce and Gabbana*. New York: Abbeville, 1996.

Sato, Kazuko. *Issey Miyake: Making Things*. Edited by Hervé Chandès. Exh. cat. New York: Scalo Publishers; Paris: Fondation Cartier pour l'art contemporain, 1999.

Settembrini, Luigi, ed. *Emilio Pucci*. Milan: Skira; Florence: Biennale di Firenze, 1996.

Shaeffer, Claire B. *Couture Sewing: Techniques*. Newtown, CT: The Taunton Press, 1994.

Shimizu, Sanae. *Unlimited: Comme des Garçons*. Tokyo: Heibonsha, 2005.

Steele, Valerie. *Fashion, Italian Style*. Exh. cat. New York: The Fashion Institute of Technology, 2003.

Steele, Valerie. *Fifty Years of Fashion: New Look to Now*. New Haven and London: Yale University Press, 1997.

Street Magazine: Maison Martin Margiela, Special Volumes 1 and 2. New York: D.A.P., 1999.

Teng, Yeohlee, et al. *Yeohlee: Work*. Mulgrave, Victoria, Australia: Peleus Press, 2003.

Vercelloni, Isa Tutino. *Krizia. A Story*. Milan: Skira, 1995.

Wilcox, Claire, ed. *Radical Fashion*. Exh. cat. New York: Abrams; London: V&A Publications, 2001.

Wilcox, Claire, ed. *Vivienne Westwood*. Exh. cat. New York: Abrams; London: V&A Publications, 2004.

Windels, Veerle. *Young Belgian Fashion Design*. Ghent and Amsterdam: Ludion, 2001.

Yamamoto, Yohji, and Kiyokazu Washida. *Yohji Yamamoto: Talking to Myself*. Göttingen, Germany: Steidl Publishing, 2002.

**Books are to be returned on or before
the last date below.**

Exhibition
Catalogue

LIBREX —

WITHDRAWN